Milwaukee Brewers 2020

A Baseball Companion

Edited by R.J. Anderson, Craig Goldstein and Bret Sayre

Baseball Prospectus

Craig Brown, Steven Goldman and David Pease, Consultant Editors
Robert Au, Harry Pavlidis and Amy Pircher, Statistics Editors

Copyright © 2020 by DIY Baseball, LLC.
All rights reserved

This book or any part thereof may not be reproduced or transmitted in any form or by any means, electronic or mechanical, including photocopying, recording, or by any information storage and retrieval system, without permission in writing from the publisher.

Limit of Liability/Disclaimer of Warranty: While the publisher and the author have used their best efforts in preparing this book, they make no representations or warranties with respect to the accuracy or completeness of the contents of this book and specifically disclaim any implied warranties of merchantability or fitness for a particular purpose. No warranty may be created or extended by sales representatives or written sales materials. The advice and strategies contained herein may not be suitable for your situation. You should consult with a professional where appropriate. Neither the publisher nor the author shall be liable for any loss of profit or any other commercial damages, including but not limited to special, incidental, consequential, or other damages.

Library of Congress Cataloging-in-Publication Data:
paperback
ISBN-13: 978-1-950716-08-1

Project Credits
Cover Design: Michael Byzewski at Aesthetic Apparatus
Interior Design and Production: Jeff Pease, Dave Pease
Layout: Jeff Pease, Dave Pease

Baseball icon courtesy of Uberux, from https://www.shareicon.net/author/uberux

Ballpark diagram courtesy of Lou Spirito/THIRTY81 Project, https://thirty81project.com/

Manufactured in the United States of America
10 9 8 7 6 5 4 3 2 1

Table of Contents

Statistical Introduction v

Part 1: Team Analysis

Milwaukee Brewers: Where Are You Going, Where Have You Been? 3
    Matthew Trueblood and Keanan Lamb
Performance Graphs 7
2019 Team Performance 8
2020 Team Projections 9
Team Personnel 10
Miller Park Stats 11
Brewers Team Analysis 13

Part 2: Player Analysis

Brewers Player Analysis 20
Brewers Prospects 95

Part 3: Featured Articles

The Baseball Is Juiced (Again) 109
    Robert Arthur
The Moral Hazard of Playing It Safe 113
    Craig Goldstein

Index of Names 119

Statistical Introduction

Sports are, fundamentally, a blend of athletic endeavor and storytelling. Baseball, like any other sport, tells its stories in so many ways: in the arc of a game from the stands or a season from the box scores, in photos, or even in numbers. At Baseball Prospectus, we understand that statistics don't replace observation or any of baseball's stories, but complement everything else that makes the game so much fun.

What stats help us with is with patterns and precision, variance and value. This book can help you learn things you may not see from watching a game or hundred, whether it's the path of a career over time or the breadth of the entire MLB. We'd also never ask you to choose between our numbers and the experience of viewing a game from the cheap seats or the comfort of your home; our publication combines running the numbers with observations and wisdom from some of the brightest minds we can find. But if you *do* want to learn more about the numbers beyond what's on the backs of player jerseys, let us help explain.

Offense

We've revised our methodology for determining batting value. Long-time readers of the book will notice that we've retired True Average in favor of a new metric: Deserved Runs Created Plus (DRC+). Developed by Jonathan Judge and our stats team, this statistic measures everything a player does at the plate–reaching base, hitting for power, making outs, and moving runners over–and puts it on a scale where 100 equals league-average performance. A DRC+ of 150 is terrific, a DRC+ of 100 is average and a DRC+ of 75 means you better be an excellent defender.

DRC+ also does a better job than any of our previous metrics in taking contextual factors into account. The model adjusts for how the park affects performance, but also for things like the talent of the opposing pitcher, value of different types of batted-ball events, league, temperature and other factors. It's able to describe a player's expected offensive contribution than any other statistic we've found over the years, and also does a better job of predicting future performance as well.

There's a lot more to DRC+'s story, and you can read all about it in greater depth near the end of this book.

Milwaukee Brewers 2020

The other aspect of run-scoring is baserunning, which we quantify using Baserunning Runs. BRR not only records the value of stolen bases (or getting caught in the act), but also accounts for all the stuff that doesn't show up on the back of a baseball card: a runner's ability to go first to third on a single, or advance on a fly ball.

Defense

Where offensive value is *relatively* easy to identify and understand, defensive value is...not. Over the past dozen years, the sabermetric community has focused mostly on stats based on zone data: a real-live human person records the type of batted ball and estimated landing location, and models are created that give expected outs. From there, you can compare fielders' actual outs to those expected ones. Simple, right?

Unfortunately, zone data has two major issues. First, zone data is recorded by commercial data providers who keep the raw data private unless you pay for it. (All the statistics we build in this book and on our website use public data as inputs.) That hurts our ability to test assumptions or duplicate results. Second, over the years it has become apparent that there's quite a bit of "noise" in zone-based fielding analysis. Sometimes the conclusions drawn from zone data don't hold up to scrutiny, and sometimes the different data provided by different providers don't look anything alike, giving wildly different results. Sometimes the hard-working professional stringers or scorers might unknowingly inflict unconscious bias into the mix: for example good fielders will often be credited with more expected outs despite the data, and ballparks with high press boxes tend to score more line drives than ones with a lower press box.

Enter our Fielding Runs Above Average (FRAA). For most positions, FRAA is built from play-by-play data, which allows us to avoid the subjectivity found in many other fielding metrics. The idea is this: count how many fielding plays are made by a given player and compare that to expected plays for an average fielder at their position (based on pitcher ground ball tendencies and batter handedness). Then we adjust for park and base-out situations.

When it comes to catchers, our methodology is a little different thanks to the laundry list of responsibilities they're tasked with beyond just, well, catching and throwing the ball. By now you've probably heard about "framing" or the art of making umpires more likely to call balls outside the strike zone for strikes. To put this into one tidy number, we incorporate pitch tracking data (for the years it exists) and adjust for important factors like pitcher, umpire, batter and home-field advantage using a mixed-model approach. This grants us a number for how many strikes the catcher is personally adding to (or subtracting from) his pitchers' performance...which we then convert to runs added or lost using linear weights.

Framing is one of the biggest parts of determining catcher value, but we also take into account blocking balls from going past, whether a scorer deems it a passed ball or a wild pitch. We use a similar approach—one that really benefits from the pitch tracking data that tells us what ends up in the dirt and what doesn't. We also include a catcher's ability to prevent stolen bases and how well they field balls in play, and *finally* we come up with our FRAA for catchers.

Pitching

Both pitching and fielding make up the half of baseball that isn't run scoring: run prevention. Separating pitching from fielding is a tough task, and most recent pitching analysis has branched off from Voros McCracken's famous (and controversial) statement, "There is little if any difference among major-league pitchers in their ability to prevent hits on balls hit in the field of play." The research of the analytic community has validated this to some extent, and there are a host of "defense-independent" pitching measures that have been developed to try and extract the effect of the defense behind a hurler from the pitcher's work.

Our solution to this quandary is Deserved Run Average (DRA), our core pitching metric. DRA looks like earned run average (ERA), the tried-and-true pitching stat you've seen on every baseball broadcast or box score from the past century, but it's very different. To start, DRA takes an event-by-event look at what the pitchers does, and adjusts the value of that event based on different environmental factors like park, batter, catcher, umpire, base-out situation, run differential, inning, defense, home field advantage, pitcher role and temperature. That mixed model gives us a pitcher's expected contribution, similar to what we do for our DRC+ model for hitters and FRAA model for catchers. (Oh, and we also consider the pitcher's effect on basestealing and on balls getting past the catcher.)

It's important to note that DRA is set to the scale of runs allowed per nine innings (RA9) instead of ERA, which makes DRA's scale slightly higher than ERA's. The reason for this is because ERA tends to overrate three types of pitchers:

1. Pitchers who play in parks where scorers hand out more errors. Official scorers differ significantly in the frequency at which they assign errors to fielders.
2. Ground-ball pitchers, because a substantial proportion of errors occur on groundballs.
3. Pitchers who aren't very good. Better pitchers often allow fewer unearned runs than bad pitchers, because good pitchers tend to find ways to get out of jams.

Since the last time you picked up an edition of this book, we've also made a few minor changes to DRA to make it better. Recent research into "tunneling"—the act of throwing consecutive pitches that appear similar from a batter's point of view until after the swing decision point–data has given us a new contextual factor to account for in DRA: plate distance. This refers to the distance between successive pitches as they approach the plate, and while it has a smaller effect than factors like velocity or whiff rate, it still can help explain pitcher strikeout rate in our model.

New Pitching Metrics for 2020

We're including a few "new" pitching metrics in the book for the 2020 edition, though unlike last year, these numbers may be a little bit more familiar to those of you who have spent some time investigating baseball statistics.

Fastball Percentage

Our fastball percentage (FB%) statistic measures how frequently a pitcher throws a pitch classified as a "fastball," measured as a percentage of overall pitches thrown. We qualify three types of fastballs:

1. The traditional four-seam fastball;
2. The two-seam fastball or sinker;
3. "Hard cutters," which are pitches that have the movement profile of a cut fastball and are used as the pitcher's primary offering or in place of a more traditional fastball.

For example, a pitcher with a FB% of 67 throws any combination of these three pitches about two-thirds of the time.

Whiff Rate

Everybody loves a swing and a miss, and whiff rate (WHF) measures how frequently pitchers induce a swinging strike. To calculate WHF, we add up all the pitches thrown that ended with a swinging strike, then divide that number by a pitcher's total pitches thrown. Most often, high whiff rates correlate with high strikeout rates (and overall effective pitcher performance).

Called Strike Probability

Called Strike Probability (CSP) is a number that represents the likelihood that all of a pitcher's pitches will be called a strike while controlling for location, pitcher and batter handedness, umpire and count. Here's how it works: on each pitch, our model determines how many times (out of 100) that a similar pitch was called for a strike given those factors mentioned above, and when normalized for each batter's strike zone. Then we average the CSP for all pitches thrown by a pitcher in a season, and that gives us the yearly CSP percentage you see in the stats boxes.

As you might imagine, pitchers with a higher CSP are more likely to work in the zone, where pitchers with a lower CSP are likely locating their pitches outside the normal strike zone, for better or for worse.

Projections

Many of you aren't turning to this book just for a look at what a player has done, but for a look at what a player is going to do: the PECOTA projections. PECOTA, initially developed by Nate Silver (who has moved on to greater fame as a political analyst), consists of three parts:

1. Major-league equivalencies, which use minor-league statistics to project how a player will perform in the major leagues;
2. Baseline forecasts, which use weighted averages and regression to the mean to estimate a player's current true talent level; and
3. Aging curves, which uses the career paths of comparable players to estimate how a player's statistics are likely to change over time.

With all those important things covered, let's take a look at what's in the book this year.

Team Prospectus

Most of this book is composed of team chapters, with one for each of the 30 major-league franchises. On the first page of each chapter, you'll see a box that contains some of the key statistics for each team as well as a very inviting stadium diagram. (You can see an example of this for the Milwaukee Brewers on this very page!)

We start with the team name, their unadjusted 2019 win-loss record, and their divisional ranking. Beneath that are a host of other team statistics. **Pythag** presents an adjusted 2019 winning percentage, calculated by taking runs scored per game (**RS/G**) and runs allowed per game (**RA/G**) for the team, and running them through a version of Bill James' Pythagorean formula that was refined and improved by David Smyth and Brandon Heipp. (The formula is called "Pythagenpat," which is equally fun to type and to say.)

Next up is **DRC+**, described earlier, to indicate the overall hitting ability of the team either above or below league-average. Run prevention on the pitching side is covered by **DRA** (also mentioned earlier) and another metric: Fielding Independent Pitching (**FIP**), which calculates another ERA-like statistic based on strikeouts, walks, and home runs recorded. Defensive Efficiency Rating (**DER**) tells us the percentage of balls in play turned into outs for the team, and is a quick fielding shorthand that rounds out run prevention.

After that, we have several measures related to roster composition, as opposed to on-field performance. **B-Age** and **P-Age** tell us the average age of a team's batters and pitchers, respectively. **Salary** is the combined team payroll for all on-field players, and Doug Pappas' Marginal Dollars per Marginal Win (**M$/MW**) tells us how much money a team spent to earn production above replacement level.

Ending this batch of statistics is the number of disabled list days a team had over the season (**IL Days**) and the amount of salary paid to players on the disabled list (**$ on IL**); this final number is expressed as a percentage of total payroll.

Next to each of these stats, we've listed each team's MLB rank in that category from first to 30th. In this, first always indicates a positive outcome and 30th a negative outcome, except in the case of salary—first is highest.

After the franchise statistics, we share a few items about the team's home ballpark. There's the aforementioned diagram of the park's dimensions (including distances to the outfield wall), a graphic showing the height of the wall from the left-field pole to the right-field pole, and a table showing three-year park factors for the stadium. The park factors are displayed as indexes where 100 is average, 110 means that the park inflates the statistic in question by 10 percent, and 90 means that the park deflates the statistic in question by 10 percent.

On the second page of each team chapter, you'll find three graphs. The first is the **2019 Hit List Ranking**. This shows our Hit List Rank for the team on each day of the 2019 season and is intended to give you a picture of the ups and downs of the team's season. Hit List Rank measures overall team performance and drives the Hit List Power Rankings at the baseballprospectus.com website.

The second graph is **Committed Payroll** and helps you see how the team's payroll has compared to the MLB and divisional average payrolls over time. Payroll figures are current as of January 1, 2020; with so many free agents still unsigned as of this writing, the final 2020 figure will likely be significantly different for many teams. (In the meantime, you can always find the most current data at Baseball Prospectus' Cot's Baseball Contracts page.)

The third graph is **Farm System Ranking** and displays how the Baseball Prospectus prospect team has ranked the organization's farm system since 2007.

After the graphs, we have a **Personnel** section that lists many of the important decision-makers and upper-level field and operations staff members for the franchise, as well as any former Baseball Prospectus staff members who are currently part of the organization. (In very rare circumstances, someone might be on both lists!)

Juan Soto LF

Born: 10/25/98 Age: 21 Bats: L Throws: L
Height: 6'1" Weight: 185 Origin: International Free Agent, 2015

YEAR	TEAM	LVL	AGE	PA	R	2B	3B	HR	RBI	BB	K	SB	CS	AVG/OBP/SLG
2017	NAT	RK	18	27	3	1	1	0	4	2	1	0	0	.320/.370/.440
2017	HAG	A	18	96	15	5	0	3	14	10	8	1	2	.360/.427/.523
2018	HAG	A	19	74	12	5	3	5	24	14	13	2	0	.373/.486/.814
2018	POT	A+	19	73	17	3	1	7	18	11	8	0	1	.371/.466/.790
2018	HAR	AA	19	35	4	2	0	2	10	4	7	1	0	.323/.400/.581
2018	WAS	MLB	19	494	77	25	1	22	70	79	99	5	2	.292/.406/.517
2019	WAS	MLB	20	659	110	32	5	34	110	108	132	12	1	.282/.401/.548
2020	WAS	MLB	21	630	92	30	3	35	102	85	123	5	2	.284/.382/.543

Comparables: Ronald Acuña Jr., Mike Trout, Tony Conigliaro

YEAR	TEAM	LVL	AGE	PA	DRC+	VORP	BABIP	BRR	FRAA	WARP
2017	NAT	RK	18	27	135	1.5	.333	0.0	RF(9): -1.1	0.0
2017	HAG	A	18	96	181	8.0	.373	1.0	RF(19): -1.9, LF(2): -0.3	0.9
2018	HAG	A	19	74	222	14.5	.405	0.3	RF(14): 1.1, CF(2): 0.2	1.2
2018	POT	A+	19	73	260	15.4	.340	1.4	RF(14): 1.0, LF(1): 0.0	1.6
2018	HAR	AA	19	35	113	3.6	.364	0.0	LF(4): 0.6, RF(4): -0.5	0.1
2018	WAS	MLB	19	494	125	40.5	.338	-0.5	LF(114): 2.7	3.0
2019	WAS	MLB	20	659	136	49.0	.312	1.4	LF(150): -0.8	4.9
2020	WAS	MLB	21	630	133	43.6	.310	-0.1	LF 3	4.8

Position Players

After all that information and a thoughtful bylined essay covering each team, we present our player comments. These are also bylined, but due to frequent franchise shifts during the offseason, our bylines are more a rough guide than a perfect accounting of who wrote what.

Each player is listed with the major-league team that employed him as of early January 2020. If a player changed teams after that point via free agency, trade, or any other method, you'll be able to find them in the chapter for their previous squad.

As an example, take a look at the player comment for Nationals outfielder Juan Soto: the stat block that accompanies his written comment is at the top of this page. First we cover biographical information (age is as of June 30, 2020) before moving onto the stats themselves. Our statistic columns include standard identifying information like **YEAR**, **TEAM**, **LVL** (level of affiliated play) and **AGE** before getting into the numbers. Next, we provide raw, untranslated numbers like you might find on the back of your dad's baseball cards: **PA** (plate appearances), **R** (runs), **2B** (doubles), **3B** (triples), **HR** (home runs), **RBI** (runs batted in), **BB** (walks), **K** (strikeouts), **SB** (stolen bases) and **CS** (caught stealing).

Next, we have unadjusted "slash" statistics: **AVG** (batting average), **OBP** (on-base percentage) and **SLG** (slugging percentage). Following the slash line is **DRC+** (Deserved Runs Created Plus), which we described earlier as total offensive expected contribution compared to the league average.

One of our oldest active metrics, **VORP** (Value Over Replacement Player), considers offensive production, position and plate appearances. In essence, it is the number of runs contributed beyond what a replacement-level player at the same position would contribute if given the same percentage of team plate appearances. VORP does not consider the quality of a player's defense.

BABIP (batting average on balls in play) tells us how often a ball in play fell for a hit, and can help us identify whether a batter may have been lucky or not...but note that high BABIPs also tend to follow the great hitters of our time, as well as speedy singles hitters who put the ball on the ground.

The next item is **BRR** (Baserunning Runs), which covers all of a player's baserunning accomplishments including (but not limited to) swiped bags and failed attempts. Next is **FRAA** (Fielding Runs Above Average), which also includes the number of games previously played at each position noted in parentheses. Multi-position players have only their two most frequent positions listed here, but their total FRAA number reflects all positions played.

Our last column here is **WARP** (Wins Above Replacement Player). WARP estimates the total value of a player, which means for hitters it takes into account hitting runs above average (calculated using the DRC+ model), BRR and FRAA. Then, it makes an adjustment for positions played and gives the player a credit for plate appearances based upon the difference between "replacement level"—which is derived from the quality of players added to a team's roster after the start of the season–and the league average.

The final line just below the stats box is **PECOTA** data, which is discussed further in a following section.

Catchers

Catchers are a special breed, and thus they have earned their own separate box which displays some of the defensive metrics that we've built just for them. As an example, let's check out J.T. Realmuto.

The **YEAR** and **TEAM** columns match what you'd find in the other stat box. **P. COUNT** indicates the number of pitches thrown while the catcher was behind the plate, including swinging strikes, fouls and balls in play. **FRM RUNS** is the total run value the catcher provided (or cost) his team by influencing the umpire to call strikes where other catchers did not. **BLK RUNS** expresses the total run value above or below average for the catcher's ability to prevent wild pitches and passed balls. **THRW RUNS** is calculated using a similar model as the previous two statistics, and it measures a catcher's ability to throw out basestealers but also to dissuade them from testing his arm in the first place. It takes into account factors like the pitcher (including his delivery and pickoff move) and baserunner (who could be as fast as Billy Hamilton or as slow as Yonder Alonso). **TOT RUNS** is the sum of all of the previous three statistics.

Justin Verlander RHP
Born: 02/20/83 Age: 37 Bats: R Throws: R
Height: 6'5" Weight: 225 Origin: Round 1, 2004 Draft (#2 overall)

YEAR	TEAM	LVL	AGE	W	L	SV	G	GS	IP	H	HR	BB/9	K/9	K	GB%	BABIP
2017	DET	MLB	34	10	8	0	28	28	172	153	23	3.5	9.2	176	34%	.283
2017	HOU	MLB	34	5	0	0	5	5	34	17	4	1.3	11.4	43	32%	.194
2018	HOU	MLB	35	16	9	0	34	34	214	156	28	1.6	12.2	290	31%	.272
2019	HOU	MLB	36	21	6	0	34	34	223	137	36	1.7	12.1	300	36%	.219
2020	HOU	MLB	37	15	6	0	29	29	184	138	28	2.3	12.1	248	35%	.274

Comparables: Zack Greinke, A.J. Burnett, Aníbal Sánchez

YEAR	TEAM	LVL	AGE	WHIP	ERA	DRA	WARP	MPH	FB%	WHF	CSP
2017	DET	MLB	34	1.28	3.82	4.03	3.0	97.7	58	11	47.8
2017	HOU	MLB	34	0.65	1.06	3.08	0.9	97.5	59.6	15.1	49.9
2018	HOU	MLB	35	0.90	2.52	2.33	7.3	97.5	61.2	16.2	51.6
2019	HOU	MLB	36	0.80	2.58	2.51	7.9	96.8	49.9	17.5	48.3
2020	HOU	MLB	37	1.01	2.75	2.95	5.3	95.8	54.6	15.1	48.2

Pitchers

Let's give our pitchers a turn, using 2019 AL Cy Young winner Justin Verlander as our example. Take a look at his stat block: the first line and the **YEAR**, **TEAM**, **LVL** and **AGE** columns are the same as in the position player example earlier.

Here too, we have a series of columns that display raw, unadjusted statistics compiled by the pitcher over the course of a season: **W** (wins), **L** (losses), **SV** (saves), **G** (games pitched), **GS** (games started), **IP** (innings pitched), **H** (hits allowed) and **HR** (home runs allowed). Next we have two statistics that are rates: **BB/9** (walks per nine innings) and **K/9** (strikeouts per nine innings), before returning to the unadjusted K (strikeouts).

Next up is **GB%** (ground ball percentage), which is the percentage of all batted balls that were hit on the ground, including both outs and hits. Remember, this is based on observational data and subject to human error, so please approach this with a healthy dose of skepticism.

BABIP (batting average on balls in play) is calculated using the same methodology as it is for position players, but it often tells us more about a pitcher than it does a hitter. With pitchers, a high BABIP is often due to poor defense or bad luck, and can often be an indicator of potential rebound, and a low BABIP may be cause to expect performance regression. (A typical league-average BABIP is close to .290-.300.)

The metrics **WHIP** (walks plus hits per inning pitched) and **ERA** (earned run average) are old standbys: WHIP measures walks and hits allowed on a per-inning basis, while ERA measures earned runs on a nine-inning basis. Neither of these stats are translated or adjusted.

DRA (Deserved Run Average) was described at length earlier, and measures how many runs the pitcher "deserved" to allow per nine innings. Please note that since we lack all the data points that would make for a "real" DRA for minor-league events, the DRA displayed for minor league partial-seasons is based off of different data. (That data is a modified version of our cFIP metric, which you can find more information about on our website.)

Just like with hitters, **WARP** (Wins Above Replacement Player) is a total value metric that puts pitchers of all stripes on the same scale as position players. We use DRA as the primary input for our calculation of WARP. You might notice that relief pitchers (due to their limited innings) may have a lower WARP than you were expecting or than you might see in other WARP-like metrics. WARP does not take leverage into account, just the actions a pitcher performs and the expected value of those actions...which ends up judging high-leverage relief pitchers differently than you might imagine given their prestige and market value.

MPH gives you the pitcher's 95th percentile velocity for the noted season, in order to give you an idea of what the *peak* fastball velocity a pitcher possesses. Since this comes from our pitch-tracking data, it is not publicly available for minor-league pitchers.

Finally, we display the three new pitching metrics we described earlier. **FB%** (fastball percentage) gives you the percentage of fastballs thrown out of all pitches. **WHF** (whiff rate) tells you the percentage of swinging strikes induced out of all pitches. **CSP** (called strike probability) expresses the likelihood of all pitches thrown to result in a called strike, after controlling for factors like handedness, umpire, pitch type, count and location.

PECOTA

All players have PECOTA projections for 2020, as well as a set of other numbers that describe the performance of comparable players according to PECOTA. All projections for 2020 are for the player at the date we went to press in early January and are projected into the league and park context as indicated by the team abbreviation. (Note that players at very low levels of the minors are too unpredictable to assess using these numbers.) All PECOTA projected statistics represent a player's projected major-league performance.

Below the projections are the player's three highest-scoring comparable players as determined by PECOTA. All comparables represent a snapshot of how the listed player was performing at the same age as the current player, so if a

23-year-old pitcher is compared to Bartolo Colón, he's actually being compared to a 23-year-old Colón, not the version that pitched for the Rangers in 2018, nor to Colón's career as a whole.

A few points about pitcher projections. First, we aren't yet projecting peak velocity, so that column will be blank in the PECOTA lines. Second, projecting DRA is trickier than evaluating past performance, because it is unclear how deserving each pitcher will be of his anticipated outcomes. However, we know that another DRA-related statistic–contextual FIP or cFIP–estimates future run scoring very well. So for PECOTA, the projected DRA figures you see are based on the past cFIPs generated by the pitcher and comparable players over time, along with the other factors described above.

Lineouts

In each chapter's Lineouts section, you'll find abbreviated text comments, as well as all the same information you'd find in our full player comments. The only difference is that we limit the stats boxes in this section to only including the 2019 information for each player.

Managers

After all those wonderful team chapters, we've got statistics for each big-league manager, all of whom are organized by alphabetical order. Here you'll find a block including an extraordinary amount of information collected from each manager's entire career. For more information on the acronyms and what they mean, please visit the Glossary at www.baseballprospectus.com.

There is one important metric that we'd like to call attention to, and you'll find it next to each manager's name: **wRM+** (weighted reliever management plus). Developed by Rob Arthur and Rian Watt, wRM+ investigates how good a manager is at using their best relievers during the moments of highest leverage, using both our proprietary DRA metric as well as Leverage Index. wRM+ is scaled to a league average of 100, and a wRM+ of 105 indicates that relievers were used approximately five percent "better" than average. On the other hand, a wRM+ of 95 would tell us the team used its relievers five percent "worse" than the average team.

While wRM+ does not have an extremely strong correlation with a manager, it is statistically significant; this means that a manager is not *entirely* responsible for a team's wRM+, but does have some effect on that number.

PECOTA Leaderboards

If you're familiar with PECOTA, then you'll have noticed that the projection system often appears bullish on players coming off a bad year and bearish on players coming off a good year. (This is because the system weights several previous seasons, not just the most recent one.) In addition, we publish the 50th

Milwaukee Brewers 2020

percentile projections for each player—which is smack in the middle of the range of projected production—which tends to mean PECOTA stat lines don't often have extreme results like 40 home runs or 250 strikeouts in a given season. In essence, PECOTA doesn't project very many extreme seasons.

At the end of the book, we've ranked the top players at each position based on their PECOTA projections. This might help you visualize just how a given player's projection compares to that of their peers, so that even if a dramatic stat line isn't projected, you can still imagine how they stack up against the rest of the league. ∎

Part 1: Team Analysis

Milwaukee Brewers: Where Are You Going, Where Have You Been?

Matthew Trueblood and Keanan Lamb

2019: What Went Right

First and foremost, and despite his regrettable season-ending injury, Christian Yelich proved that his emergence as perhaps the best player in the National League in the second half of 2018 was no fluke. Yelich led the National League in DRC+, stole 30 bases in 32 tries, and came up with the big hit seemingly every time one was needed. Yelich had five tying or go-ahead hits in the ninth inning or extras, tying him for the league lead. He won the triple-slash triple crown, leading the NL in batting average, on-base percentage, and slugging average, something last done by Miguel Cabrera in 2013 (and last done on the senior circuit by Barry Bonds in 2004). PECOTA only projected him to bat .277/.353/.466, which was plainly too low, but no projection system could have credibly forecast .329/.429/.671, and that's where he finished.

To support their superstar, Milwaukee made offseason mini-splurges on Mike Moustakas and Yasmani Grandal. A qualifying offer hampered Grandal's market, and Moustakas remained of disturbingly little interest on the open market, so each came to the team on a one-year deal for less than $20 million. For that meager buck, they got an overwhelming bang. Grandal turned in 6.1 WARP, playing nearly every day and posting a 124 DRC+ on the strength of 28 home runs and 109 walks. He also became the linchpin of their run-prevention plan, delivering his usual sterling work as a pitch-framer. Moustakas posted his third straight season of roughly three wins, whacking 35 homers and playing adequate defense at two infield positions.

When the team's other options at second base fell apart, Keston Hiura came up and had a sensational rookie season. If anything, Hiura's DRC+ of 115 understates the jolt he gave to the team's offense throughout the second half. Despite some down years from more established players, the team cobbled together a solid offensive attack.

On the other side of the ledger, the team kept doing some of the things that allowed them to surge so impressively at the end of 2018. Only the Orioles had a higher Defensive Efficiency on fly balls, and that's only because almost every fly ball the Orioles allowed flew over the wall, thereby not being counted among balls in play. Lorenzo Cain, though obviously playing through a number of nagging injuries, captained the best defensive outfield in the majors.

Josh Hader was less unhittable than he'd been in 2018 but was still one of the two or three most dominant relievers in baseball. Offseason pickup Alex Claudio helped stabilize the middle relief corps, within which Junior Guerra also stepped up and delivered important, solid innings. At the trade deadline, David Stearns and his staff correctly identified Drew Pomeranz as a potentially dominant short-burst reliever. In the final month, manager Craig Counsell saw past the underwhelming stuff of Brent Suter and turned him into a solid reliever, too.

Despite an oblique injury that interrupted his breakout campaign, Brandon Woodruff stepped up and became the reliable top-of-the-rotation arm the team desperately needed him to be. His stuff has always been solid, but his command was sharper for most of 2019 than it had ever been before, and the result was 3.4 WARP in just 122 innings, not including his four overpowering frames in the Wild Card game. The team also signed Gio González when he opted out of a minor-league deal with the Yankees, and he delivered the same low-volume, low-wattage, high-value performance for them in 2019 that he's delivered to them and to the Nationals throughout his gentle, elongated decline phase.

2019: What Went Wrong

As good as Hader was, the rest of the pitching staff largely fell apart. Letting Wade Miley go to Houston in free agency—for very little money— was a mistake. Jhoulys Chacin found that there is a point of diminishing returns, and even a point at which returns become negative where slider usage is concerned; he went from staff ace to unusable relatively quickly. Freddy Peralta and Corbin Burnes flashed the ability to dominate, but (to different degrees) proved unable to get outs consistently. Jeremy Jeffress never looked like the pitcher who shut opponents down throughout 2018. He and Corey Knebel, who underwent Tommy John surgery, left gaping holes in the bullpen.

Travis Shaw and Jesús Aguilar regressed badly after strong showings in 2018 and had to be replaced in the starting lineup. Cain's age (and the physical toll of his style of play) showed much more than it had in 2018, especially at the plate. Orlando Arcia has now been given three years' worth of opportunities to demonstrate competence as an everyday shortstop and he's failed to do so.
—Matthew Trueblood

Prospect Outlook

The state of the farm might not be loaded with near-ready talent, but the recent graduations of Keston Hiura and Trent Grisham are a sign of a healthy player development program and baseball ops department. Their contributions were undoubtedly critical to the Brewers playoff run following the Yelich injury. There are still concerns about Hiura's long-term defensive viability, as well as whether Grisham can maintain his offensive momentum following his swing change this season. However, if their progress is any indication, the likes of shortstop **Brice Turang**, catcher **Mario Feliciano**, and outfielder **Tristen Lutz** will benefit greatly as they move up the ranks as both are several years away from readiness.

The Brewers have recently made a habit of turning their better upper-level pitching prospects into bullpen studs—think of Josh Hader, Freddy Peralta, Jimmy Nelson, and Corbin Burnes. Next in line is power-arm **Drew Rasmussen**, with command/control-types **Zack Brown** and recent draftee **Ethan Small** raising questions about their ultimate role given their profiles. Beyond that, it's a fairly shallow system in need of restocking, a challenge that management has proven they are quite capable of meeting. —*Keanan Lamb*

2020 Outlook

While they've been opportunistic and aggressive in recent winters and at trade deadlines, the David Stearns-led front office still faces pressure to think and behave like a small-market team. They largely did so this winter. No one can accuse Stearns of being passive, and each of his moves makes sense, but taken together, the offseason has the feel of having shopped in the bargain bin, and that will be the aesthetic of the team come Opening Day.

Gone are Moustakas, Grandal, Chase Anderson, Jordan Lyles, Eric Thames, Travis Shaw, Gio González, Pomeranz, and Jeffress. Gone, too, via trade, is Grisham; Stearns swapped Grisham and Davies to San Diego in a deal that brought him Luis Urías, who he hopes can be the team's medium-term answer at shortstop (pending recovery from a late-winter broken left hamate). He also traded for Grandal's replacement, acquiring Omar Narváez from the Mariners. Then came a slew of free-agent deals, mostly at very low salaries that preserve the flexibility the team cultivated over the previous few seasons. Avisaíl García was willing to sign with the team despite their already crowded outfield, suggesting that Counsell will continue to use his bench and rotate players out of the lineup for rest as frequently as any manager in baseball. García, Justin Smoak, and Eric Sogard all signed knowing they were likely to be platooned, but still have good chances to play often. Jedd Gyorko and Ryon Healy have tougher paths to playing time, but also had fewer alternatives, so the Brewers and Counsell held sufficient appeal.

Milwaukee Brewers 2020

Brett Anderson and Josh Lindblom were inexpensive but fit the profiles of pitchers with whom the Brewers have had excellent luck lately. Eric Lauer, who came over in the Urías deal, is similarly underwhelming, yet effective. Milwaukee is starting to lean heavily toward a stars-and-scrubs roster construction, but through excellent management and instruction, they have demonstrated the ability to get more out of their supporting cast than that label suggests.
—Matthew Trueblood

Performance Graphs

2019 Hit List Ranking

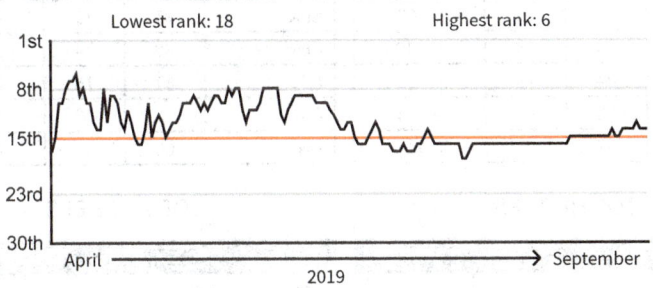

Committed Payroll (in millions)

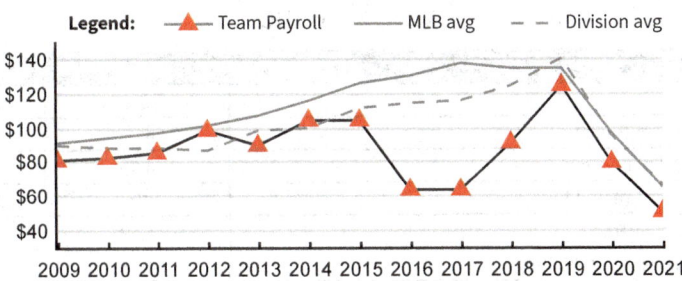

Farm System Ranking

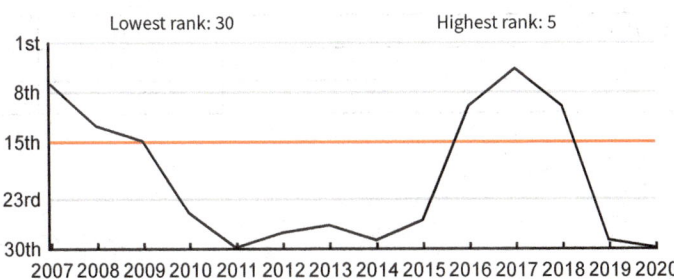

2019 Team Performance

ACTUAL STANDINGS

Team	W	L	Pct
SLN	91	71	0.562
MIL	**89**	**73**	**0.549**
CHN	84	78	0.519
CIN	75	87	0.463
PIT	69	93	0.426

THIRD-ORDER STANDINGS

Team	W	L	Pct
SLN	91	71	0.564
CHN	88	74	0.543
MIL	**87**	**75**	**0.535**
CIN	86	76	0.534
PIT	66	96	0.407

TOP HITTERS

Player	WARP
Christian Yelich	6.5
Yasmani Grandal	6.1
Mike Moustakas	2.9

TOP PITCHERS

Player	WARP
Brandon Woodruff	3.4
Josh Hader	2.6
Adrian Houser	2.5

VITAL STATISTICS

Statistic Name	Value	Rank
Pythagenpat	.502	15th
Runs Scored per Game	4.75	15th
Runs Allowed per Game	4.73	15th
Deserved Runs Created Plus	97	14th
Deserved Run Average	4.59	11th
Fielding Independent Pitching	4.41	16th
Defensive Efficiency Rating	.708	12th
Batter Age	28.9	27th
Pitcher Age	28.6	19th
Salary	$123.4M	17th
Marginal $ per Marginal Win	$2.7M	24th
Injured List Days	1060	15th
$ on IL	11%	5th

2020 Team Projections

PROJECTED STANDINGS

Team	W	L	Pct	+/-
CIN	86.1	75.9	0.531	11
CHN	84.5	77.5	0.522	0
SLN	80.3	81.7	0.496	-11
MIL	**79.4**	**82.6**	**0.490**	**-10**
PIT	70.3	91.7	0.434	1

TOP PROJECTED HITTERS

Player	WARP
Christian Yelich	5.0
Lorenzo Cain	2.4
Luis Urías	1.8

TOP PROJECTED PITCHERS

Player	WARP
Brandon Woodruff	3.1
Josh Hader	1.9
Freddy Peralta	1.0

FARM SYSTEM REPORT

Top Prospect	Number of Top 101 Prospects
Brice Turang	0

KEY DEDUCTIONS

Player	WARP
Yasmani Grandal	5.9
Mike Moustakas	2.0
Travis Shaw	1.4
Trent Grisham	1.0
Eric Thames	0.9
Gio Gonzalez	0.7
Zach Davies	0.7
Chase Anderson	0.4
Drew Pomeranz	0.3
Jordan Lyles	0.3

KEY ADDITIONS

Player	WARP
Luis Urías	1.8
Eric Sogard	1.5
Avisaíl García	1.0
Omar Narváez	0.9
Eric Lauer	0.9
Josh Lindblom	0.6
Brett Anderson	0.5
Justin Smoak	0.4
J.P. Feyereisen	0.4
Brock Holt	0.3

Team Personnel

President - Baseball Operations and General Manager
David Stearns

Senior Vice President and Assistant General Manager
Matt Arnold

Senior Vice President - Player Personnel
Karl Mueller

Manager
Craig Counsell

BP Alumni
James Fisher
Adam Hayes
Greg Goldstein
Mike Groopman
Shawn Hoffman
Matt Kleine
Dan Turkenkopf

Miller Park Stats

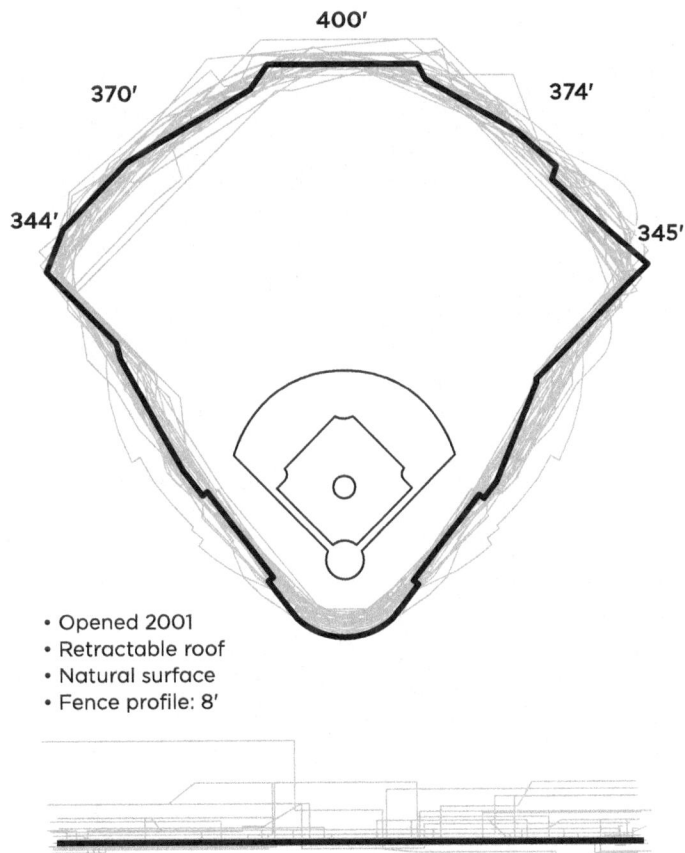

- Opened 2001
- Retractable roof
- Natural surface
- Fence profile: 8'

Three-Year Park Factors

Runs	Runs/RH	Runs/LH	HR/RH	HR/LH
102	103	101	104	105

Miller Park Stats

Three-Year Park Factors

Brewers Team Analysis

We think about fandom as something static and binary: you either are or are not a baseball fan. But that's not really accurate. Fandom often waxes and wanes. In baseball, it is reconstituted every spring as people choose to become invested again and choose to expend time, money and emotional energy on their favorite team. As Major League Baseball continues to tinker with countless rules—to try and fix what's ostensibly wrong with baseball—in order to attract new fans, it often seems as if the current baseball fan is left unexplored or taken for granted.

What is it about baseball that refuses to allow millions of people to let the sport go? Instead of taking established fandom as an immutable given, Major League Baseball should talk and listen to current fans—in part to avoid losing their base, and in part because such efforts are likely helpful in MLB's commitment to growth. The things that current fans love about the game can be improved upon and/or better leveraged to incorporate more potential fans.

For example, baseball attracts the analytical types. Whether we talk about Strat-O-Matic debuting in the early 1960s, the emergence of Baseball Prospectus in 1996 or Sony Pictures bankrolling a $50 million movie in 2011 about the sabermetric revolution, it's almost banal at this point to point out how baseball fandom has long been correlated with those who harbor an affinity for numbers. It's clear that Major League Baseball is leaning into this appeal with Statcast and analytics-driven television broadcasts. They've even hired sabermetrically inclined writers, like Mike Petriello, to drive these types of fans to the league's website more often.

After interviewing roughly two dozen Milwaukee Brewers fans, though, a very different theme emerges regarding fandom: community. Diehard fans treasure the various kinds of personal connections that they find through baseball.

The desire for community stands out because Americans voluntarily come together in society less than ever before. Political scientist Robert Putnam famously wrote about the decline of social interaction in Bowling Alone (2000). In his study, Putnam charts less engagement in civic and religious organizations, and the title comes from the odd fact that the number of Americans who bowl has increased while activity in bowling leagues has dropped. American society, according to Putnam, has become more individualized. Historian Daniel Rodgers agrees with Putnam and argued that Americans' social and communal ways of understanding the world have been replaced over the last four or five decades with language and metaphors that stress individualism, agency, and choice. Rodgers calls this the Age of Fracture.[1]

In Wisconsin and beyond, the Milwaukee Brewers appear to help counter this age of fracture. "The second I find out another person is a Brewers fan," Brad Ford explained, "we immediately have a connection that makes it so easy to build a friendship." Relationships are built over an extended period of time, with small common experiences being stacked upon one another until there's something stable on which to stand. Baseball fandom provides a shortcut. As Jason Spitz told me, "I love feeling like I'm part of an experience that can't fully be grasped by outsiders." For many who love baseball, fandom is relational. No fan spoke to me about their love of the Brewers without mentioning how it tied them to other people, even (and sometimes especially) strangers.

If Putnam and Rodgers are correct that American society is fracturing and becoming more individualized, baseball and other sports might serve as one of the last widespread avenues for large-scale community engagement. And Brewers fans, at least, love the game for that fact.

Sometimes that community looks like throngs of people grilling brats, drinking beer and playing catch in the stadium parking lots. Though tailgating may be popular for football games across the country, it happens in earnest 81 times a year for baseball games in Wisconsin. Paul Noonan said, "With pace-of-play and the length of games being top of mind for everyone else, Milwaukeeans are happy to add a few extra hours to every game, and occasionally, not make it in until the third." In other words, going to a baseball game is often just an excuse to clear the schedule, leave work behind, and get both friends and family together at the ballpark.

Sometimes that community looks like 40,000-plus people cheering for the blue and gold inside Miller Park itself. For Aaron Sevedge, it "warms his soul" when he thinks of the strong local support the Brewers have, "even after 20 years in the playoff wilderness." It's an expression of civic pride, of communal support for something beyond the individual. Mike Treacy explained that his love for baseball developed when he was young and attended games at old County Stadium in Milwaukee. It wasn't the product on the field that attracted him, as the Brewers compiled a losing record in every season between 1993 and 2004, but the atmosphere drew him in. "At that age, I didn't care" about wins and losses, Treacy said, "baseball games were fun to go to." Talking to Brewers fans, it was common to learn that their love of baseball developed from physically attending games. There was something special and engrossing about sitting in the bleachers with thousands of like-minded individuals, cheering for the same outcome.

Sometimes, though, that community proved to be much smaller than thousands of strangers in a single stadium. The Brewers have knitted families together over time. Trenni Kusnierek, now an anchor and sports reporter for NBC Sports Boston, explained that being a Brewers fan was just part of growing up in her family. Even when the Brewers made the NLCS in 2018, Kusnierek said that she flew home to take her brother and sister to Game 6. She then went to Game 7 with her mom and dad. Supporting the Brewers was fundamentally a family affair. That is also true for Jason Spitz. He has always shared the Brewers with his family—first his dad and brother, now with his wife and kids.

That community regularly crosses generational lines, too. When Brewers fans told stories about their family, they involved parents, children, grandchildren, nieces, and nephews. It was never just about brothers, sisters or cousins. Beyond extended families, though, Sean Andrews explained that he enjoys being a part of a fanbase that can boast distinct generations with different experiences. The CC Sabathia trade in 2008 made Sean a supporter of the team, but he values the "older, hardcore crowd who were around for the '82 team." America has always dealt with intergenerational conflict—with the "OK Boomer" meme being its latest manifestation—but it's significant that baseball, in part, holds meaning for many Brewers fans because it brings together people of all ages.

Whether it centered on tailgating, attending games, uniting families or overcoming generational divides, the clearest common theme that emerged when talking to Brewers supporters about their fandom was community.

⚾ ⚾ ⚾

However, if what diehard Brewers fans cherish most about their fandom, and what often drew them into baseball in the first place, is the communal aspect of the game, both the league and its franchises appear to be shooting themselves in the foot.

According to the *New York Times*, Major League Baseball has suffered a 14-percent drop in ticket sales since 2007, which works out to roughly 11 million fewer tickets sold.[2] Part of this is because teams are diversifying their revenue streams and are less reliant on getting butts in seats to prop up their bottom line. Teams like the Los Angeles Angels, on the other hand, have also recognized that they can increase their profits, despite lower attendance numbers, as long as they attract the right kind of fan (i.e., a wealthier fan who can spend more money at the ballpark).[3] This latter trend of increasing ticket prices with an eye toward the economic quality of a baseball fan, rather than the quantity of fans, explains why teams may not be worried about the short-term consequences of decreased attendance.

What's undeniable, though, is that such trends are crippling the very thing that Brewers fans claim to value most.

Decreasing access to live baseball extends down to the minor leagues. Numerous reports have suggested that Major League Baseball and Minor League Baseball plan to contract up to 42 current minor-league affiliates.[4] The league has claimed that such streamlining will eliminate the organizations that have inadequate facilities, and it will also enable minor-league players to receive higher pay. Putting aside the various structural, economic and moral critiques that can be leveled at such an argument, slashing almost four dozen minor-league clubs will remove even more opportunities for baseball to attract new fans via the kinds of communal activities described above. This is especially true for potential baseball fans in less populated parts of the country, creating what could be described as more of an urban-rural divide in access to live baseball.

It is also important to ask for whom these baseballing communities have been built. Major League Baseball has catered to mostly cisgender, heterosexual white men throughout its history, including in the 21st century, and those cultural biases have often sheltered and sustained various kinds of abuse, harassment, discrimination, and disparate access. For baseball to truly be a positive communal force, as many Brewers fans suggest it could be, Major League Baseball must meaningfully address these prejudices and blindspots. There are positive steps being made on which MLB can build, such as the Play Ball initiative and MLB's partnership with mitú. And while commissioner Rob Manfred has pushed to grow the game among African-American communities, Latinx communities, women and younger generations, more effort must be concentrated in these directions and beyond.

There is a dissonance between Major League Baseball's perpetual desire to grow the game and access new markets, and their recent actions. They are eliminating its best chance at organic growth in the United States. The league is sometimes limiting access to games through higher prices and uneven support of diversity, while other times removing access to live baseball altogether. If sustained fandom is created through involvement in baseballing communities, it is difficult to see from where this engagement comes with the current trends. Even worse, it stands to figure that Major League Baseball might be pushing away current baseball fans by curtailing their favorite part of the game.

The Brewers are better off, in some respects, than many other teams when it comes to creating communities at Miller Park. They're consistently a top-half team in terms of attendance, despite being located in the league's smallest metropolitan market.[5] This is due to three reasons: (1) the team ranks in the league's top-10 most affordable stadiums;[6] (2) Miller Park's roof enables long-term planning for families; and (3) tailgating. The latter point deserves special mention. Multiple fans swore the tailgating experience couldn't be disentangled from the game itself; they were one and the same. Those people are saying something about what's important to them—being allowed to drink before noon for afternoon games, as one fan said, but also that baseball fandom is more meaningful with other people.

As Major League Baseball caters to what it thinks younger baseball fans want—better technology, more statistics, faster games, and more balls in play—it should also ask what attracted current fans in the first place. Growing the game is impossible if baseball is not able to retain its current fanbase. Listening to Brewers fans, the league should be accommodating and creating opportunities for physical community whenever possible, not limiting them. Major League Baseball may ultimately be chasing its own tail if it pursues higher profits and new markets by undercutting—and fracturing—what made it successful in the first place.

—*J.P. Breen is an author of Baseball Prospectus.*

1. Robert D. Putnam, *Bowling Alone: The Collapse and Revival of American Community*. New York: Simon & Schuster Paperbacks, 2000; Daniel T. Rodgers, *Age of Fracture*. Cambridge, Mass.: Belknap Press of Harvard University Press, 2011.

2. https://www.nytimes.com/2019/09/29/sports/baseball/mlb-attendance.html

3. https://www.ocregister.com/2015/06/04/moura-angels-see-fewer-fans-but-revenue-rises-with-higher-ticket-prices/

4. https://www.baseballamerica.com/stories/mlb-floats-proposal-that-would-eliminate-42-minor-league-teams/

5. https://www.baseball-almanac.com/articles/baseball_markets.shtml

6. https://finance.yahoo.com/news/most-least-expensive-stadiums-mlb-090700815.html

Part 2: Player Analysis

PLAYER COMMENTS WITH GRAPHS

Orlando Arcia SS
Born: 08/04/94   Age: 25   Bats: R   Throws: R
Height: 6'0"   Weight: 165   Origin: International Free Agent, 2010

YEAR	TEAM	LVL	AGE	PA	R	2B	3B	HR	RBI	BB	K	SB	CS	AVG/OBP/SLG
2017	MIL	MLB	22	548	56	17	2	15	53	36	100	14	7	.277/.324/.407
2018	CSP	AAA	23	96	16	5	1	2	8	10	15	2	1	.341/.417/.494
2018	MIL	MLB	23	366	32	16	0	3	30	15	87	7	4	.236/.268/.307
2019	MIL	MLB	24	546	51	16	1	15	59	43	109	8	5	.223/.283/.350
2020	MIL	MLB	25	210	20	9	1	5	22	14	44	5	2	.234/.288/.371

Comparables: Pete Runnels, Ketel Marte, Francisco Lindor

There was a time when Arcia was projected to become a No. 2 hitter with a well-above-average glove at short. That hasn't happened, least of all on the offensive end. He continued to struggle at the plate last season—though he did improve his exit velocity and walked more often without seeing bottom-line improvement—and his glove grew more spotty as the season burned on—perhaps a sign he was taking his issues into the field with him. As a result, the Brewers benched Arcia in favor of Tyler Saladino, of all people. Arcia will probably get another chance to prove he's the cat's meow, but maybe not in Milwaukee—they acquired Luis Urías to slot in at short.

YEAR	TEAM	LVL	AGE	PA	DRC+	VORP	BABIP	BRR	FRAA	WARP
2017	MIL	MLB	22	548	94	26.1	.317	2.1	SS(152): 6.8	3.0
2018	CSP	AAA	23	96	127	10.8	.397	2.3	SS(22): 3.9	1.4
2018	MIL	MLB	23	366	59	-0.1	.305	2.0	SS(116): 3.8	0.4
2019	MIL	MLB	24	546	74	7.9	.253	-0.7	SS(150): -2.3	0.5
2020	MIL	MLB	25	210	74	0.9	.275	0.5	SS 2, 3B 0	0.3

Orlando Arcia, continued

Batted Ball Distribution

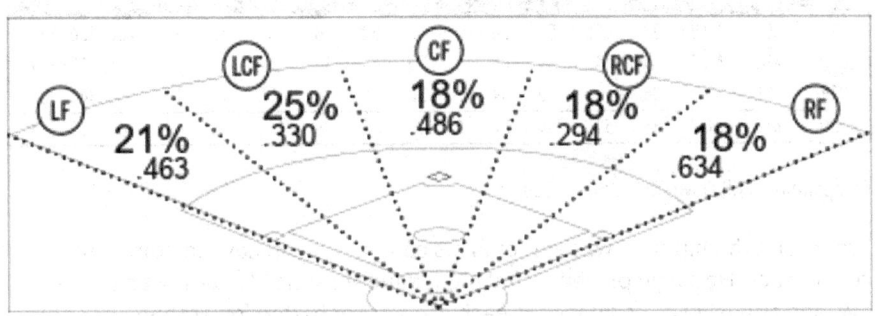

Strike Zone vs LHP   **Strike Zone vs RHP**

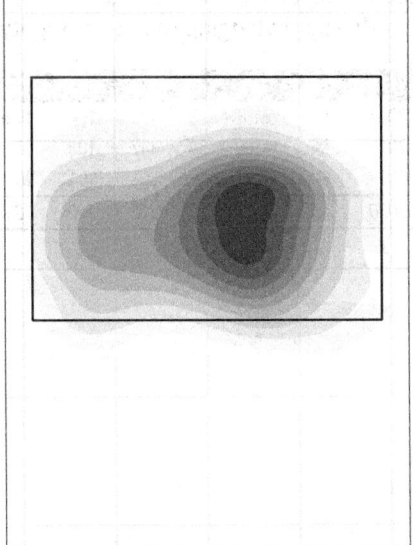

Ryan Braun LF

Born: 11/17/83   Age: 36   Bats: R   Throws: R
Height: 6'2"   Weight: 205   Origin: Round 1, 2005 Draft (#5 overall)

YEAR	TEAM	LVL	AGE	PA	R	2B	3B	HR	RBI	BB	K	SB	CS	AVG/OBP/SLG
2017	MIL	MLB	33	425	58	28	2	17	52	38	76	12	4	.268/.336/.487
2018	MIL	MLB	34	447	59	25	1	20	64	34	85	11	5	.254/.313/.469
2019	MIL	MLB	35	508	70	31	2	22	75	34	105	11	1	.285/.343/.505
2020	MIL	MLB	36	518	64	27	2	24	73	38	114	13	4	.262/.323/.475

Comparables: Cliff Floyd, Tim Wallach, George Hendrick

Braun isn't the hitter he was earlier in his career, but you have to admire his consistency. He's now played 13 full big-league seasons, delivering an above-average offensive performance in each. He's never batted lower than .250; he's reached base more often than 32 percent of the time all but once; and his lowest slugging percentage is .453. He's done all this while switching positions as often as the Brewers desired. The drug-test scandal is a permanent blemish on Braun's record, but as he enters the final guaranteed year of his contract, it's worth acknowledging that it's a mighty fine record, as far as ballplaying goes.

YEAR	TEAM	LVL	AGE	PA	DRC+	VORP	BABIP	BRR	FRAA	WARP
2017	MIL	MLB	33	425	104	19.5	.292	0.5	LF(95): -3.7	1.0
2018	MIL	MLB	34	447	108	17.8	.274	-0.8	LF(93): -4.9, 1B(18): -0.4	0.8
2019	MIL	MLB	35	508	111	20.9	.325	0.7	LF(110): -7.1, RF(2): -0.2	1.4
2020	MIL	MLB	36	518	107	18.0	.299	0.0	LF -4, 1B 0	1.5

Ryan Braun, continued

Batted Ball Distribution

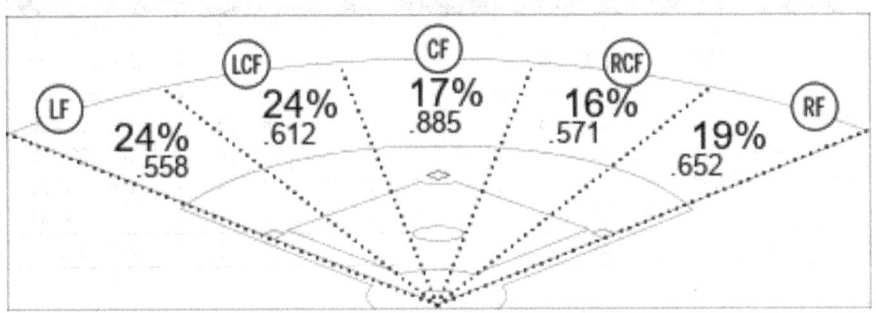

Strike Zone vs LHP   **Strike Zone vs RHP**

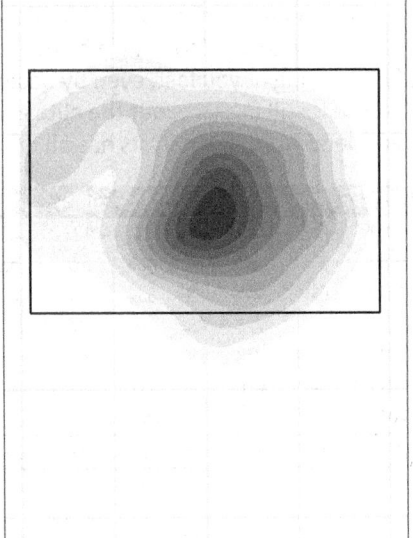

Keon Broxton CF

Born: 05/07/90 Age: 30 Bats: R Throws: R
Height: 6'3" Weight: 195 Origin: Round 3, 2009 Draft (#95 overall)

YEAR	TEAM	LVL	AGE	PA	R	2B	3B	HR	RBI	BB	K	SB	CS	AVG/OBP/SLG
2017	CSP	AAA	27	34	4	2	0	1	7	7	8	4	0	.385/.500/.577
2017	MIL	MLB	27	463	66	15	4	20	49	40	175	21	7	.220/.299/.420
2018	CSP	AAA	28	334	47	16	2	10	37	30	119	27	4	.254/.323/.421
2018	MIL	MLB	28	89	15	2	2	4	11	11	28	5	1	.179/.281/.410
2019	NYN	MLB	29	53	5	1	0	0	2	4	22	4	1	.143/.208/.163
2019	BAL	MLB	29	112	14	3	0	4	9	8	49	4	1	.204/.261/.350
2019	SEA	MLB	29	63	5	0	0	2	5	8	33	2	4	.115/.238/.231
2020	MIL	MLB	30	35	4	1	0	1	4	3	15	2	1	.201/.286/.363

Comparables: Aaron Altherr, Larry Doby, Tommy Pham

Modern baseball teams may have an increased willingness to overlook a hitter's high strikeout totals if there are rosterable secondary skills present, but Broxton's astronomical whiff rates appear to be testing the league's patience. It took five months for the outfielder to go from "Acquired for Three Players By a Team Trying to Win" to "DFA'd by the Orioles," which is a pretty devastating case of life coming at you fast, even by baseball standards. The stellar outfield defense is still in place, but the elite exit velocity that once gave hope to peripheral-hunting analysts has all but vanished.

YEAR	TEAM	LVL	AGE	PA	DRC+	VORP	BABIP	BRR	FRAA	WARP
2017	CSP	AAA	27	34	127	4.0	.500	0.5	CF(7): -0.8	0.2
2017	MIL	MLB	27	463	76	16.9	.323	3.6	CF(139): -8.2	-0.2
2018	CSP	AAA	28	334	83	10.2	.382	5.1	CF(61): -1.0, LF(8): 2.0	1.1
2018	MIL	MLB	28	89	77	6.1	.217	2.3	CF(24): 1.5, RF(20): 0.6	0.5
2019	NYN	MLB	29	53	48	-1.7	.259	-0.2	LF(18): 0.9, CF(9): 0.8	0.0
2019	BAL	MLB	29	112	39	-4.9	.340	1.5	CF(36): 5.8	0.2
2019	SEA	MLB	29	63	28	-3.7	.211	-0.2	CF(20): -0.6, LF(3): -0.2	-0.5
2020	MIL	MLB	30	35	71	0.2	.340	0.2	CF 0	0.0

Keon Broxton, continued

Batted Ball Distribution

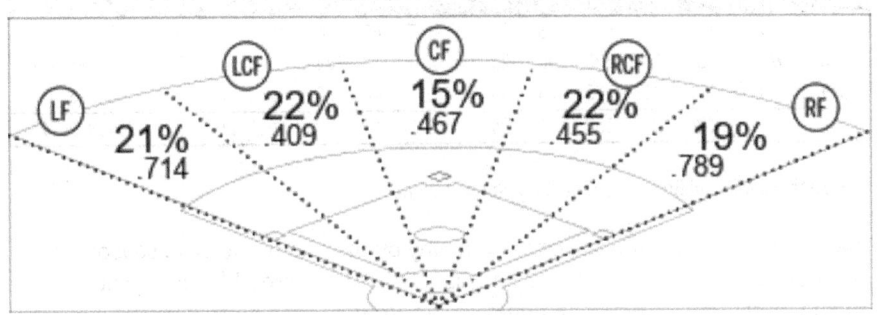

Strike Zone vs LHP

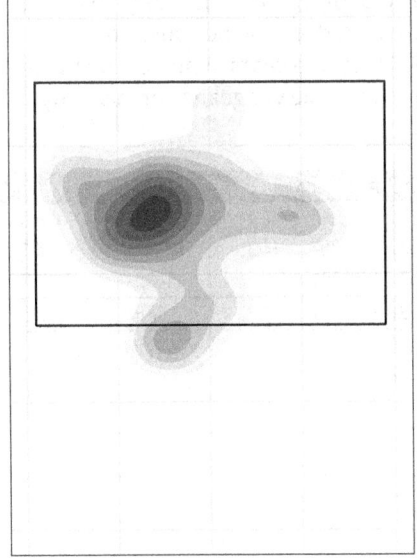

Strike Zone vs RHP

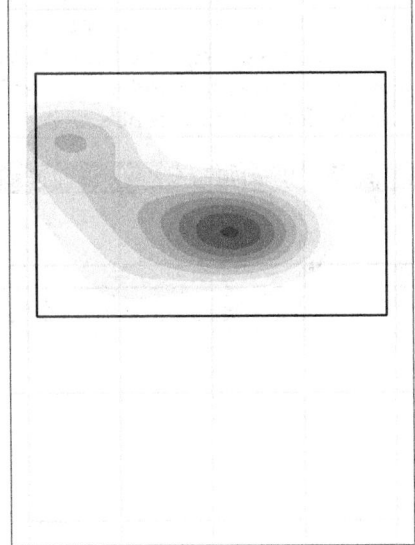

Lorenzo Cain CF

Born: 04/13/86   Age: 34   Bats: R   Throws: R
Height: 6'2"   Weight: 205   Origin: Round 17, 2004 Draft (#496 overall)

YEAR	TEAM	LVL	AGE	PA	R	2B	3B	HR	RBI	BB	K	SB	CS	AVG/OBP/SLG
2017	KCA	MLB	31	645	86	27	5	15	49	54	100	26	2	.300/.363/.440
2018	MIL	MLB	32	620	90	25	2	10	38	71	94	30	7	.308/.395/.417
2019	MIL	MLB	33	623	75	30	0	11	48	50	106	18	8	.260/.325/.372
2020	MIL	MLB	34	560	59	26	2	13	59	44	105	19	5	.264/.330/.395

Comparables: Michael Bourn, Roberto Kelly, Rondell White

It was downright painful to watch Cain play by the end of the 2019 season. It's not that he wasn't producing—Cain was reliable for incredible diving catches and an intelligent, gap-to-gap line-drive approach at the plate—but by September, he was playing through numerous ailments to the joints in both legs. A sprained ankle suffered in a collision with Rockies catcher Tony Wolters in a play at the plate during Game 161 added further insult to...well, injury. Nevertheless, when the Brewers took the field for the National League Wild Card Game, there was Cain out in center, hobbled but doing all he could do. You can't question Cain's effort, but as he enters the last three years of his contract with Milwaukee, it's fair to wonder if Father Time will take vengeance on his body sevenfold for all the miles he's racked up.

YEAR	TEAM	LVL	AGE	PA	DRC+	VORP	BABIP	BRR	FRAA	WARP
2017	KCA	MLB	31	645	119	37.2	.340	2.4	CF(151): 19.4	6.0
2018	MIL	MLB	32	620	121	53.6	.357	4.3	CF(138): 2.1	4.5
2019	MIL	MLB	33	623	87	12.8	.301	1.0	CF(143): -1.6	1.2
2020	MIL	MLB	34	560	94	18.0	.311	1.2	CF 8	2.6

Lorenzo Cain, continued

Batted Ball Distribution

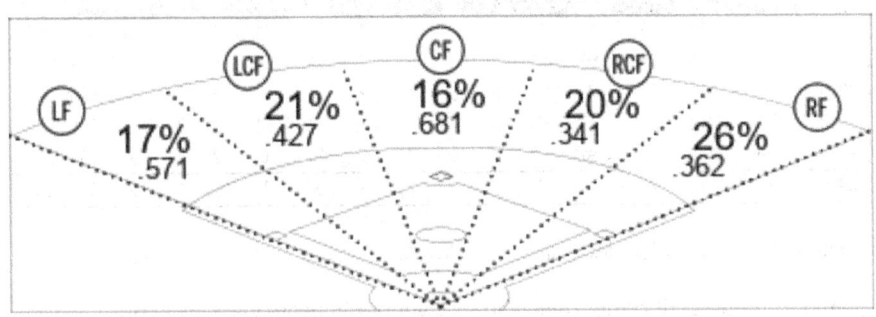

Strike Zone vs LHP

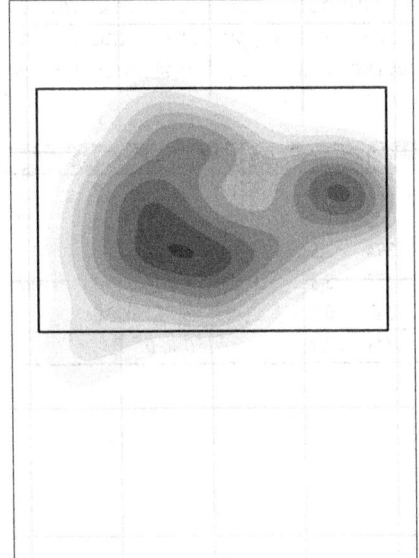

Strike Zone vs RHP

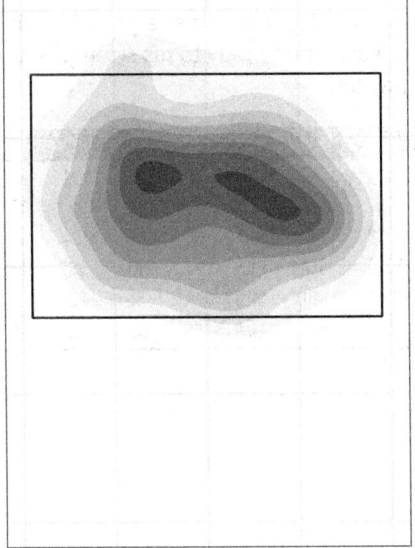

Ben Gamel OF

Born: 05/17/92   Age: 28   Bats: L   Throws: L
Height: 5'11"   Weight: 185   Origin: Round 10, 2010 Draft (#325 overall)

YEAR	TEAM	LVL	AGE	PA	R	2B	3B	HR	RBI	BB	K	SB	CS	AVG/OBP/SLG
2017	TAC	AAA	25	75	6	1	1	1	8	12	11	1	1	.300/.427/.400
2017	SEA	MLB	25	550	68	27	5	11	59	36	122	4	1	.275/.322/.413
2018	TAC	AAA	26	94	19	8	3	1	16	10	12	4	0	.349/.415/.554
2018	SEA	MLB	26	293	37	14	4	1	19	31	61	7	3	.272/.358/.370
2019	MIL	MLB	27	356	47	18	0	7	33	40	104	2	2	.248/.337/.373
2020	MIL	MLB	28	84	8	3	0	2	8	8	22	1	1	.237/.312/.367

Comparables: Jake Marisnick, Alex Presley, Bob Borkowski

Gamel remains underwhelming—he's a tweener in more ways than one—when examined without context. But within the context of the 2019 Brewers it's fair to write he was a good fit. There, he could sub in as a defensive or baserunning upgrade over Ryan Braun or Eric Thames, and could do so without embarrassing himself at the plate, the way most fourth or fifth outfielders do. Force Gamel into an everyday role and everyone is going to be miserable; put him on the bench and ask him to play to his strengths and everyone is happy. Sometimes, it's just that simple.

YEAR	TEAM	LVL	AGE	PA	DRC+	VORP	BABIP	BRR	FRAA	WARP
2017	TAC	AAA	25	75	114	6.2	.347	0.6	RF(11): -0.2, CF(7): -0.9	0.2
2017	SEA	MLB	25	550	90	12.9	.340	1.1	LF(85): -3.5, RF(50): 3.1	0.7
2018	TAC	AAA	26	94	134	10.7	.394	2.5	LF(8): -0.7, CF(6): -0.1	0.8
2018	SEA	MLB	26	293	98	12.2	.352	3.3	LF(48): -1.4, RF(40): -1.9	0.7
2019	MIL	MLB	27	356	82	2.1	.347	0.5	LF(70): -1.6, RF(23): 0.0	0.1
2020	MIL	MLB	28	84	83	0.7	.313	0.3	LF 0, RF 0	0.0

Ben Gamel, continued

Batted Ball Distribution

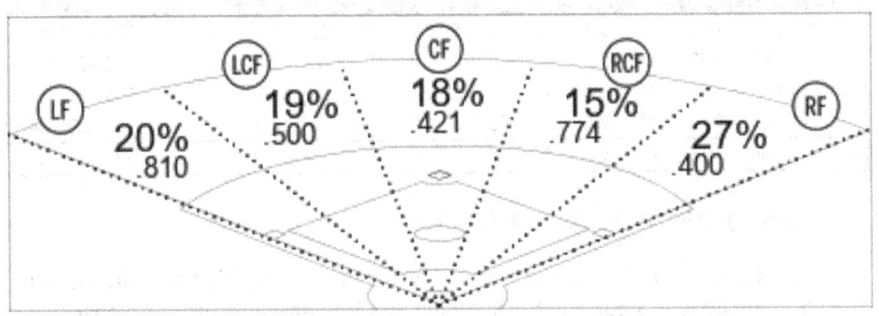

Strike Zone vs LHP   Strike Zone vs RHP

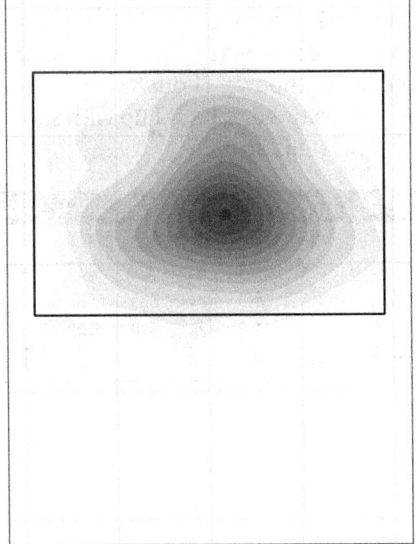

Avisaíl García   RF

Born: 06/12/91   Age: 29   Bats: R   Throws: R
Height: 6'4"   Weight: 250   Origin: International Free Agent, 2007

YEAR	TEAM	LVL	AGE	PA	R	2B	3B	HR	RBI	BB	K	SB	CS	AVG/OBP/SLG
2017	CHA	MLB	26	561	75	27	5	18	80	33	111	5	3	.330/.380/.506
2018	CHR	AAA	27	28	5	3	0	3	9	3	9	0	0	.360/.429/.840
2018	CHA	MLB	27	385	47	11	2	19	49	20	102	3	1	.236/.281/.438
2019	TBA	MLB	28	530	61	25	2	20	72	31	125	10	4	.282/.332/.464
2020	MIL	MLB	29	392	47	18	1	16	53	24	99	4	2	.271/.326/.464

Comparables: Laynce Nix, Jeff Francoeur, Dave Parker

Much like Eminem or Ron Artest, García has matured since his time with Detroit. The 28-year-old was a bargain for the Rays as a free agent signing at a base salary of $3.5 million, and even as he earned another million in plate appearance bonuses. For that modest amount, the Rays received above-average offensive production, which allowed them to cover injuries in the outfield and rotate tired players through the designated hitter spot. Despite his large frame, García's 20 home runs in 2019 represented a career high. And despite putting up unexpected reverse splits last year, he will make his biggest mark as a hired gun versus southpaws. Though with an average-ish glove and no standout tool, he seems destined to be set up with short-term relationships for the next few years until his skills atrophy.

YEAR	TEAM	LVL	AGE	PA	DRC+	VORP	BABIP	BRR	FRAA	WARP
2017	CHA	MLB	26	561	126	30.2	.392	-0.5	RF(132): 7.2	3.7
2018	CHR	AAA	27	28	138	4.9	.462	-0.3	RF(5): -0.2	0.1
2018	CHA	MLB	27	385	98	4.1	.271	-1.4	RF(87): 6.3	1.2
2019	TBA	MLB	28	530	103	14.4	.340	-3.5	RF(92): -3.7, CF(12): 2.1	0.9
2020	MIL	MLB	29	392	106	12.5	.331	-1.4	LF, CF 0	1.3

Avisaíl García, continued

Batted Ball Distribution

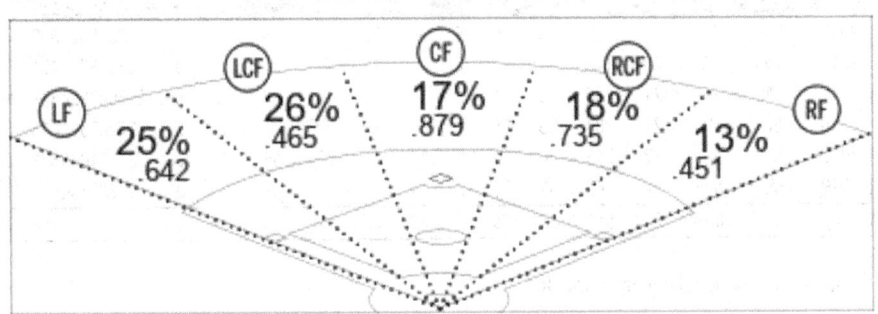

Strike Zone vs LHP

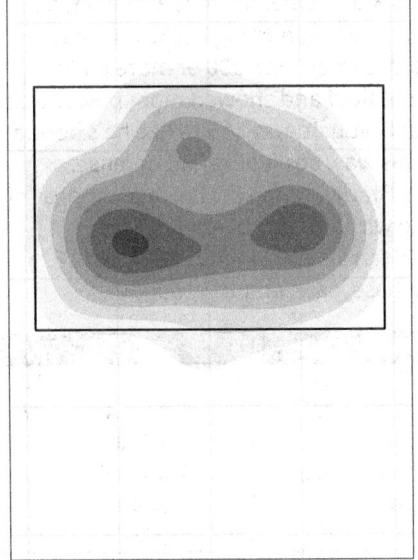

Strike Zone vs RHP

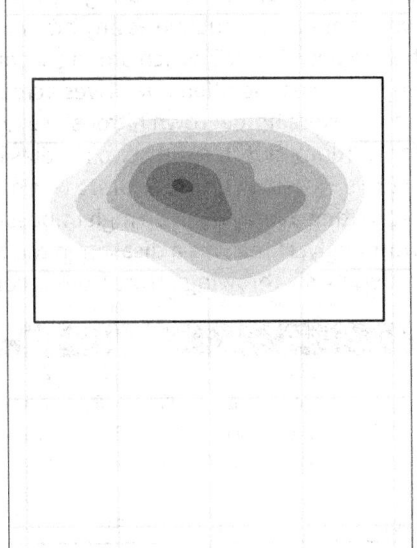

Milwaukee Brewers 2020

Keston Hiura 2B

Born: 08/02/96   Age: 23   Bats: R   Throws: R
Height: 5'11"   Weight: 190   Origin: Round 1, 2017 Draft (#9 overall)

YEAR	TEAM	LVL	AGE	PA	R	2B	3B	HR	RBI	BB	K	SB	CS	AVG/OBP/SLG
2017	BRR	RK	20	72	18	3	5	4	18	6	13	0	2	.435/.500/.839
2017	WIS	A	20	115	14	11	2	0	15	7	24	2	0	.333/.374/.476
2018	CAR	A+	21	228	38	16	3	7	23	14	47	4	6	.320/.382/.529
2018	BLX	AA	21	307	36	18	2	6	20	22	56	11	5	.272/.339/.416
2019	SAN	AAA	22	243	44	16	1	19	46	23	64	7	2	.329/.407/.681
2019	MIL	MLB	22	348	51	23	2	19	49	25	107	9	3	.303/.368/.570
2020	MIL	MLB	23	560	64	26	3	22	73	37	167	8	4	.251/.315/.444

Comparables: Frank Bolling, Ian Happ, Ted Lepcio

The Brewers resisted calling up Hiura as long as they could—presumably in part to game his service-time clock—but the struggles of Travis Shaw forced their hand. Sometimes rookies stumble out of the gate, or require extra seasoning before living up to the scouting report. Not Hiura. When he made contact, he was about as productive as any hitter in the league, posting a .268 ISO that trailed only Derek Dietrich among second basemen with 300 or more plate appearances. He rifled line drives across the field and showed more power than any Brewers homegrown hitter since Ryan Braun. It may sound like he's bound for stardom, but there are two hurdles in his way: strikeouts and defense. Hiura's 30 percent strikeout rate was more Branyan than Braun, and a repeat of his batting average will be nigh impossible without improvement. More worryingly, Hiura was a disaster in the field; errors rarely tell a story, but 16, including six throwing errors from second base, says nothing good.

YEAR	TEAM	LVL	AGE	PA	DRC+	VORP	BABIP	BRR	FRAA	WARP
2017	BRR	RK	20	72	231	17.3	.500	0.5		1.0
2017	WIS	A	20	115	138	10.4	.422	1.1	2B(3): -0.4	0.7
2018	CAR	A+	21	228	163	20.8	.386	0.6	2B(15): 0.6	1.9
2018	BLX	AA	21	307	118	13.9	.323	0.6	2B(64): -3.5	1.2
2019	SAN	AAA	22	243	155	34.3	.389	0.0	2B(46): -1.6	2.1
2019	MIL	MLB	22	348	115	18.2	.402	-0.5	2B(81): -4.9	1.3
2020	MIL	MLB	23	560	98	20.5	.330	-0.7	2B -6	1.5

Keston Hiura, continued

Batted Ball Distribution

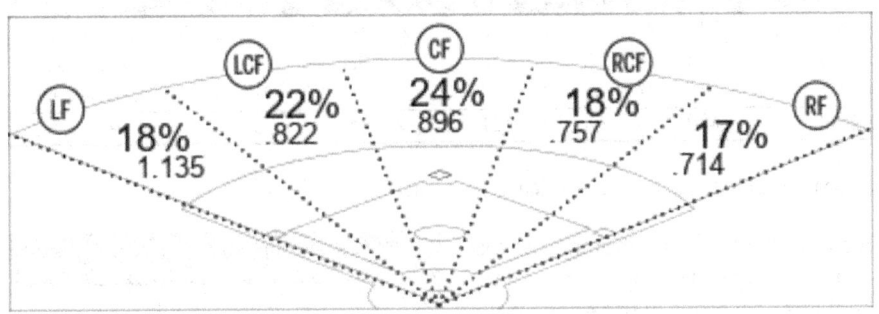

Strike Zone vs LHP

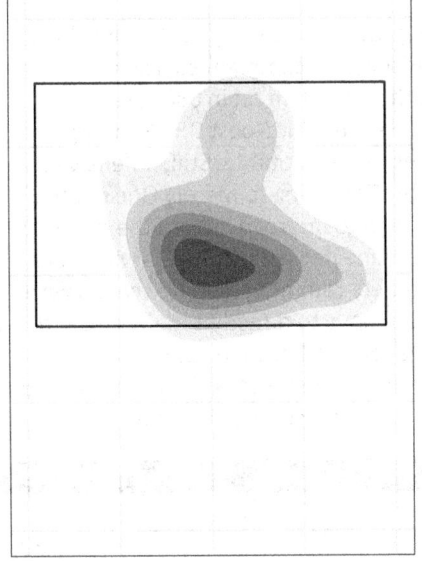

Strike Zone vs RHP

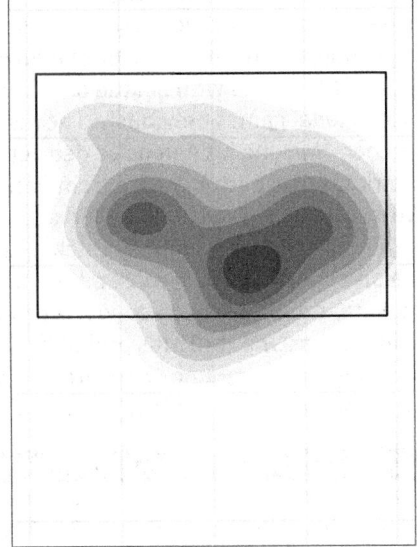

Omar Narváez C

Born: 02/10/92   Age: 28   Bats: L   Throws: R
Height: 5'11"   Weight: 220   Origin: International Free Agent, 2008

YEAR	TEAM	LVL	AGE	PA	R	2B	3B	HR	RBI	BB	K	SB	CS	AVG/OBP/SLG
2017	CHA	MLB	25	295	23	10	0	2	14	38	45	0	0	.277/.373/.340
2018	CHA	MLB	26	322	30	14	1	9	30	38	65	0	2	.275/.366/.429
2019	SEA	MLB	27	482	63	12	0	22	55	47	92	0	0	.278/.353/.460
2020	MIL	MLB	28	490	57	21	0	17	61	49	90	1	0	.269/.345/.433

Comparables: Tucker Barnhart, Russell Martin, Yorvit Torrealba

A career-high 91 starts behind the dish further exposed Narváez as one of the shakiest backstops in the game, but his defensive transgressions were masked by his progression as one of baseball's best-hitting catchers. Narváez was one of the many

YEAR	TEAM	P. COUNT	FRM RUNS	BLK RUNS	THRW RUNS	TOT RUNS
2017	CHA	11422	-6.3	-1.5	-0.6	-9.3
2018	CHA	11231	-10.8	-4.6	-0.1	-15.7
2019	SEA	13756	-8.2	-4.3	-1.0	-13.7
2020	MIL	20469	-10.8	-3.6	-1.5	-15.8

beneficiaries of a livelier baseball in 2019, although pointing to the ball alone may undersell just how drastic of a power surge he experienced: His home run total in 132 games with Seattle outpaced the 19 he had hit in 680 career professional games previously. The result was the third-best DRC+ among catchers, making his defensive deficiencies more palatable. Still, defensive metrics suggest he upgraded from Probably The Worst to merely One of the Worst catchers in the league. Narváez's efforts to improve behind the plate weren't helped by seemingly catching someone new every day; Narváez set a major-league record for most different pitchers caught in a single season with 41. Forty-one! How many co-workers do you have to directly collaborate with on a regular basis? Is it 41? It's probably a smaller number than 41. For Narváez, meetings on the mound were often quite literally just that. And now, as a reward for his success, he'll get to memorize a new set of faces in Milwaukee.

YEAR	TEAM	LVL	AGE	PA	DRC+	VORP	BABIP	BRR	FRAA	WARP
2017	CHA	MLB	25	295	100	8.6	.330	-1.0	C(83): -9.5, 1B(1): 0.0	0.4
2018	CHA	MLB	26	322	109	21.0	.330	0.0	C(85): -17.6	0.0
2019	SEA	MLB	27	482	123	37.2	.306	-1.5	C(98): -12.3, 2B(1): 0.0	2.3
2020	MIL	MLB	28	490	109	28.5	.304	-0.6	C -17	1.2

Omar Narváez, continued

Batted Ball Distribution

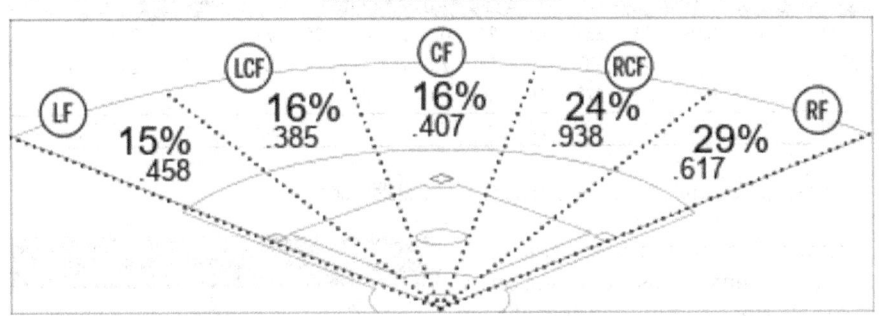

Strike Zone vs LHP   **Strike Zone vs RHP**

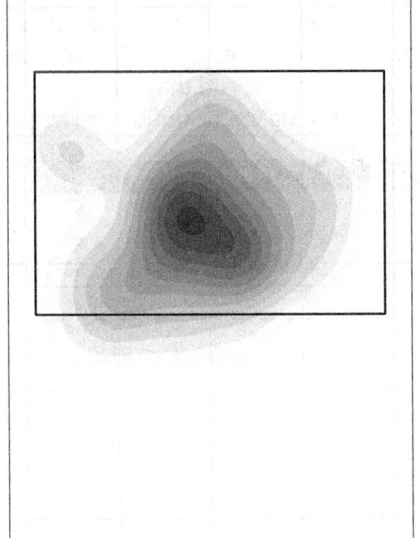

Manny Piña C

Born: 06/05/87   Age: 33   Bats: R   Throws: R
Height: 6'0"   Weight: 215   Origin: International Free Agent, 2004

YEAR	TEAM	LVL	AGE	PA	R	2B	3B	HR	RBI	BB	K	SB	CS	AVG/OBP/SLG
2017	MIL	MLB	30	359	45	21	0	9	43	20	79	2	0	.279/.327/.424
2018	MIL	MLB	31	337	39	13	2	9	28	21	62	2	0	.252/.307/.395
2019	MIL	MLB	32	179	10	8	0	7	25	16	50	0	0	.228/.313/.411
2020	MIL	MLB	33	189	20	8	0	6	23	14	47	1	0	.240/.306/.404

Comparables: Francisco Cervelli, Dioner Navarro, Martín Maldonado

Even with Piña on the wrong side of 30, and coming off his worst season at the plate since coming to Milwaukee in 2016, the Brewers continue to believe in his defensive chops. Baseball Prospectus co-founder Rany Jazayerli once suggested every backup catcher will hit .300 in a season given enough opportunity. The first half of Piña's 2017—when he hit .287/.328/.457—suggests Jazayerli had a point. Piña hasn't hit so well since, and that's all right given his defense and low cost. Much like that new song on the radio, the key to enjoying Piña is to avoid overexposure.

YEAR	TEAM	P. COUNT	FRM RUNS	BLK RUNS	THRW RUNS	TOT RUNS
2017	MIL	12774	-2.9	0.7	2.0	3.0
2018	MIL	12411	4.8	1.3	0.5	6.3
2019	MIL	6195	6.4	2.0	-0.1	8.3
2020	MIL	5531	0.3	0.5	-0.3	0.5

YEAR	TEAM	LVL	AGE	PA	DRC+	VORP	BABIP	BRR	FRAA	WARP
2017	MIL	MLB	30	359	93	16.4	.339	-0.6	C(102): 1.4	1.5
2018	MIL	MLB	31	337	90	9.1	.285	-3.6	C(92): 7.0, 1B(1): 0.0	1.6
2019	MIL	MLB	32	179	90	6.7	.284	-0.5	C(53): 8.3, 3B(1): 0.0	1.4
2020	MIL	MLB	33	189	88	4.0	.294	-0.8	C 1, 1B 0	0.5

Manny Piña, continued

Batted Ball Distribution

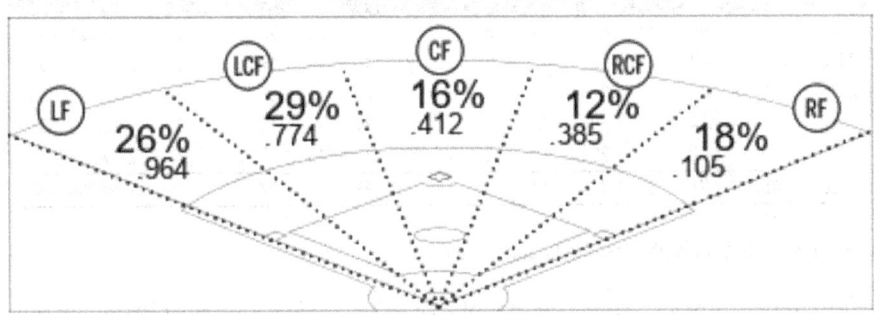

Strike Zone vs LHP   **Strike Zone vs RHP**

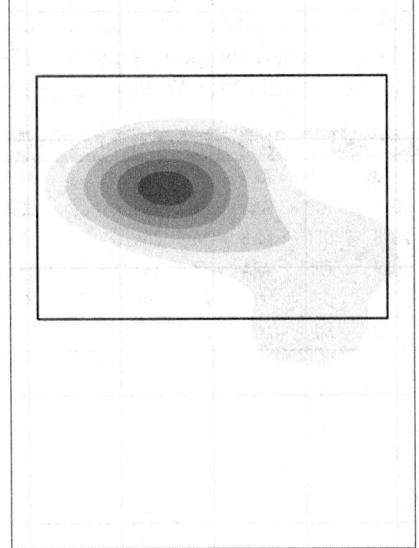

Ronny Rodríguez INF

Born: 04/17/92 Age: 28 Bats: R Throws: R
Height: 6'0" Weight: 200 Origin: International Free Agent, 2011

YEAR	TEAM	LVL	AGE	PA	R	2B	3B	HR	RBI	BB	K	SB	CS	AVG/OBP/SLG
2017	COH	AAA	25	483	60	18	2	17	64	23	92	15	5	.291/.324/.454
2018	TOL	AAA	26	275	42	20	5	9	40	10	47	10	8	.338/.365/.558
2018	DET	MLB	26	206	17	7	0	5	20	10	42	2	0	.220/.256/.335
2019	TOL	AAA	27	181	33	9	2	11	31	6	41	5	0	.320/.343/.587
2019	DET	MLB	27	294	29	12	3	14	43	13	82	3	1	.221/.252/.438
2020	MIL	MLB	28	140	17	6	1	8	22	6	37	2	1	.249/.284/.490

Comparables: Trevor Plouffe, Jose Pirela, Jimmy Paredes

Rodríguez's game aspires to be that of a Quad-A cult favorite. His big personality fits in the game; his swing-and-miss penchant doesn't. (Or, given the recent trends, maybe it does?) He will always have a spot on a team due to his joie de vivre and his infield versatility, coupled with the fact that pitchers often throw fastballs and Rodríguez has a way of turning some of those fastballs into home runs. With his not-so-secret passion of being a musician, it would be nice to see El Felino have a complete season of 25-30 home runs then write music about how he once did that. You'd do the same thing.

YEAR	TEAM	LVL	AGE	PA	DRC+	VORP	BABIP	BRR	FRAA	WARP
2017	COH	AAA	25	483	108	11.1	.329	-1.4	2B(62): 7.9, 3B(25): 1.6	3.2
2018	TOL	AAA	26	275	163	30.8	.383	-1.8	3B(34): 2.1, SS(26): -0.9	2.7
2018	DET	MLB	26	206	77	-4.4	.253	-0.3	SS(24): -2.3, 2B(17): 0.1	-0.3
2019	TOL	AAA	27	181	136	13.3	.361	-1.0	2B(24): 3.2, 3B(7): -0.5	1.3
2019	DET	MLB	27	294	72	-0.8	.254	-1.1	2B(31): 1.3, SS(20): -2.0	-0.3
2020	MIL	MLB	28	140	96	3.2	.284	-0.4	2B 1, SS 0	0.4

Ronny Rodríguez, continued

Batted Ball Distribution

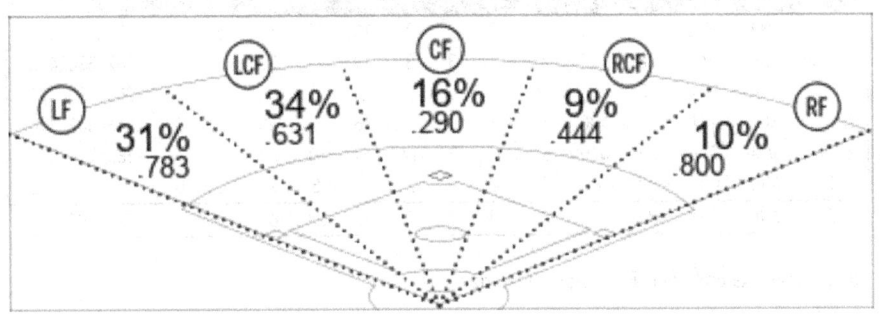

Strike Zone vs LHP   **Strike Zone vs RHP**

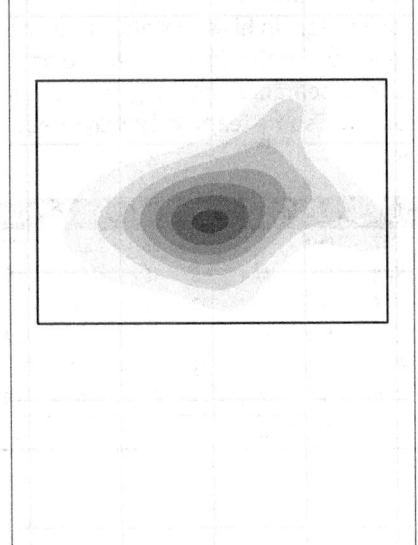

Tyler Saladino UT

Born: 07/20/89   Age: 30   Bats: R   Throws: R
Height: 6'0"   Weight: 200   Origin: Round 7, 2010 Draft (#218 overall)

YEAR	TEAM	LVL	AGE	PA	R	2B	3B	HR	RBI	BB	K	SB	CS	AVG/OBP/SLG
2017	CHA	MLB	27	281	23	9	2	0	10	23	67	5	4	.178/.254/.229
2018	CSP	AAA	28	154	23	4	3	3	19	21	28	10	0	.262/.370/.408
2018	CHA	MLB	28	9	2	1	0	0	0	0	3	0	0	.250/.250/.375
2018	MIL	MLB	28	130	11	3	0	5	16	9	38	2	2	.246/.302/.398
2019	SAN	AAA	29	310	51	19	2	17	64	41	67	8	1	.287/.384/.566
2019	MIL	MLB	29	71	7	0	0	2	8	5	26	2	0	.123/.197/.215
2020	MIL	MLB	30	251	27	9	1	9	29	21	69	8	3	.221/.291/.384

Comparables: Aaron Boone, Brock Holt, Chris Truby

You've undoubtedly heard about the Peter principle. Allow us to introduce the Pete Kozma principle, which states that a career can be extended by unreal lengths just because somebody can kinda-sorta passably play shortstop. Despite reintroducing a leg kick in the minors, Saladino was one of baseball's worst hitters in his short time in the majors. To be clear: he's always been ineffectual at the dish, but this go around he fanned in nearly 40 percent of his plate appearances, making him even more of a black hole. Fortunately for Saladino, some team will always need a shortstop. For 2020, it's the Samsung Lions.

YEAR	TEAM	LVL	AGE	PA	DRC+	VORP	BABIP	BRR	FRAA	WARP
2017	CHA	MLB	27	281	57	-14.1	.242	1.1	2B(26): 1.2, 3B(22): 4.3	0.0
2018	CSP	AAA	28	154	101	8.9	.310	1.6	SS(25): -2.6, 2B(9): -0.7	0.5
2018	CHA	MLB	28	9	80	0.0	.400	0.0	3B(2): 0.2	0.0
2018	MIL	MLB	28	130	88	3.9	.316	0.1	SS(28): 1.7, 2B(6): 0.0	0.5
2019	SAN	AAA	29	310	137	26.5	.322	0.4	LF(18): -1.0, SS(18): -1.8	2.0
2019	MIL	MLB	29	71	60	-0.9	.162	0.8	SS(13): -0.1, LF(7): -0.4	-0.1
2020	MIL	MLB	30	251	78	1.9	.276	1.1	SS 0, 2B 1	0.3

Tyler Saladino, continued

Batted Ball Distribution

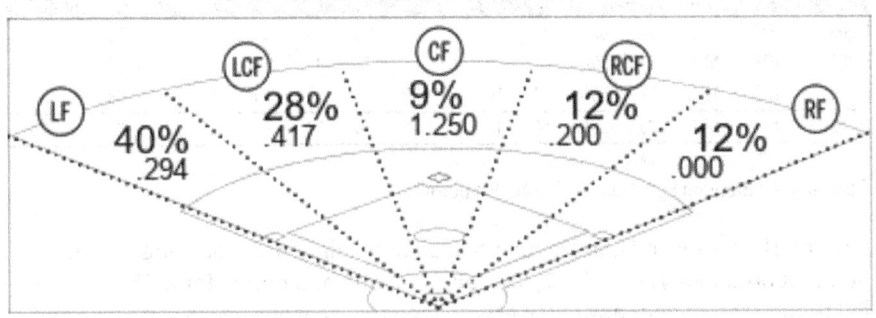

Strike Zone vs LHP   **Strike Zone vs RHP**

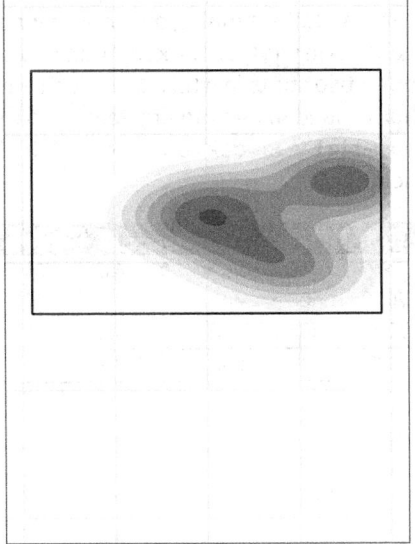

Justin Smoak 1B

Born: 12/05/86 Age: 33 Bats: B Throws: L
Height: 6'4" Weight: 220 Origin: Round 1, 2008 Draft (#11 overall)

YEAR	TEAM	LVL	AGE	PA	R	2B	3B	HR	RBI	BB	K	SB	CS	AVG/OBP/SLG
2017	TOR	MLB	30	637	85	29	1	38	90	73	128	0	1	.270/.355/.529
2018	TOR	MLB	31	594	67	34	0	25	77	83	156	0	1	.242/.350/.457
2019	TOR	MLB	32	500	54	16	0	22	61	79	106	0	0	.208/.342/.406
2020	MIL	MLB	33	399	50	16	0	18	54	54	97	1	0	.221/.332/.430

Comparables: Brandon Belt, Franklin Stubbs, Pat Burrell

2019 marked a second consecutive season of decline for Smoak after he finally had that breakout year in 2017, long after anyone had hoped for it. The average fell though the patient approach established two seasons ago was maintained, resulting in a career-best strikeout-to-walk ratio. Though he fell just two plate appearances short of qualifying for a batting title he wasn't within kilometers of, the first baseman still provided presence and consistency to a club that had little of either. In fact, Smoak grew enough on Jays fans in his five years there to earn multiple standing ovations in what was potentially his last game at Rogers Centre. He wryly remarked, "Can you believe they do that for a .200 hitter?" The other two stints in which Smoak hit within ten points of .200 (2010 and 2014) both ended in him moving teams, so misleading batting average or not, it's possible the Smoak coming out of the Sistine Chapel to herald his next deal is not Blue.

YEAR	TEAM	LVL	AGE	PA	DRC+	VORP	BABIP	BRR	FRAA	WARP
2017	TOR	MLB	30	637	135	27.4	.285	0.6	1B(151): -0.9	3.6
2018	TOR	MLB	31	594	117	14.7	.297	-5.1	1B(134): -7.2	0.8
2019	TOR	MLB	32	500	111	15.0	.223	-2.0	1B(89): -5.5	0.7
2020	MIL	MLB	33	399	104	8.8	.253	-1.1	1B -3	0.6

Justin Smoak, continued

Batted Ball Distribution

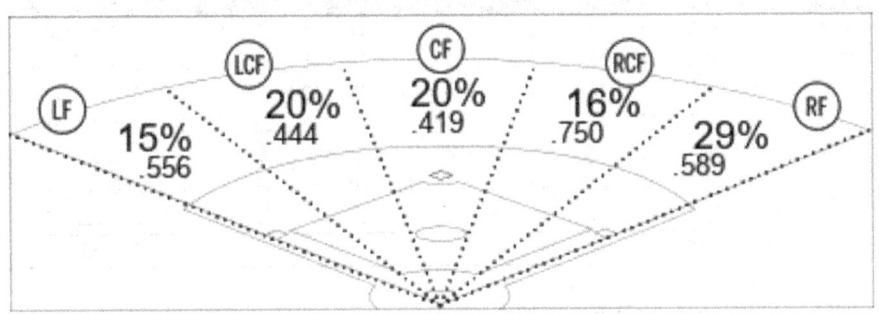

Strike Zone vs LHP   **Strike Zone vs RHP**

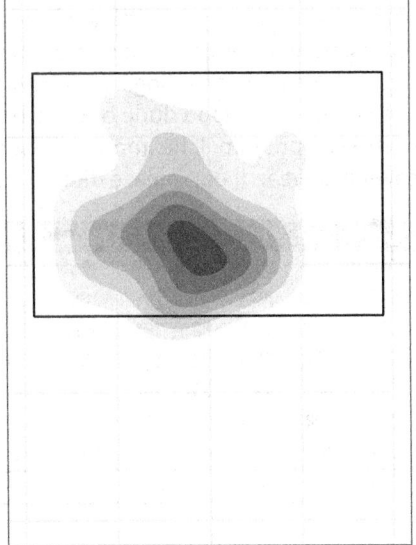

Eric Sogard 2B

Born: 05/22/86 Age: 34 Bats: L Throws: R
Height: 5'10" Weight: 185 Origin: Round 2, 2007 Draft (#81 overall)

YEAR	TEAM	LVL	AGE	PA	R	2B	3B	HR	RBI	BB	K	SB	CS	AVG/OBP/SLG
2017	CSP	AAA	31	107	30	8	0	3	17	15	12	5	0	.330/.421/.516
2017	MIL	MLB	31	299	37	15	1	3	18	45	37	3	3	.273/.393/.378
2018	CSP	AAA	32	101	10	4	0	0	11	10	16	0	1	.225/.297/.270
2018	MIL	MLB	32	113	7	3	0	0	2	12	23	3	0	.134/.241/.165
2019	BUF	AAA	33	38	7	2	0	1	6	7	4	0	0	.267/.395/.433
2019	TOR	MLB	33	323	45	17	2	10	30	29	47	6	0	.300/.363/.477
2019	TBA	MLB	33	119	14	6	0	3	10	9	16	2	0	.266/.328/.404
2020	MIL	MLB	34	497	52	24	1	11	53	48	79	7	3	.257/.333/.391

Comparables: Mark Ellis, Jim Morrison, Cliff Pennington

It is a giant upset that Sogard—the poster boy of "nerd power"—is also not the cover boy of the "nerd bible." A useful reserve for most of his career because of his defensive flexibility, Sogard did that thing where you change the angle of your launch and started hitting dingers. The 13 home runs he hit in 2019 represented 54 percent of his career total and were potentially career-saving. Without the new stick, Sogard offers little in tangible items. He has cool glasses and seems like a good dude but is average or below as a defender no matter where you put him. If he improves upon his 2019, he should probably be on the cover next year. If not, please direct all complaints to @cdgoldstein on Twitter.

YEAR	TEAM	LVL	AGE	PA	DRC+	VORP	BABIP	BRR	FRAA	WARP
2017	CSP	AAA	31	107	126	7.0	.351	-0.2	2B(15): -0.2, 3B(3): 0.0	0.6
2017	MIL	MLB	31	299	105	13.4	.311	-2.9	2B(60): -2.1, SS(26): -0.2	0.7
2018	CSP	AAA	32	101	65	-2.0	.267	1.6	2B(18): 1.2, SS(5): 1.2	0.3
2018	MIL	MLB	32	113	72	-5.4	.173	0.3	SS(24): 0.0, 2B(22): 0.1	0.1
2019	BUF	AAA	33	38	119	3.0	.269	0.7	3B(5): 0.6, 2B(2): 0.4	0.3
2019	TOR	MLB	33	323	112	14.9	.326	3.0	2B(43): -1.4, RF(6): 0.3	1.7
2019	TBA	MLB	33	119	104	4.6	.289	-0.1	2B(31): 0.7	0.5
2020	MIL	MLB	34	497	96	10.5	.291	-0.1	3B 5, 2B 0	1.7

Eric Sogard, continued

Batted Ball Distribution

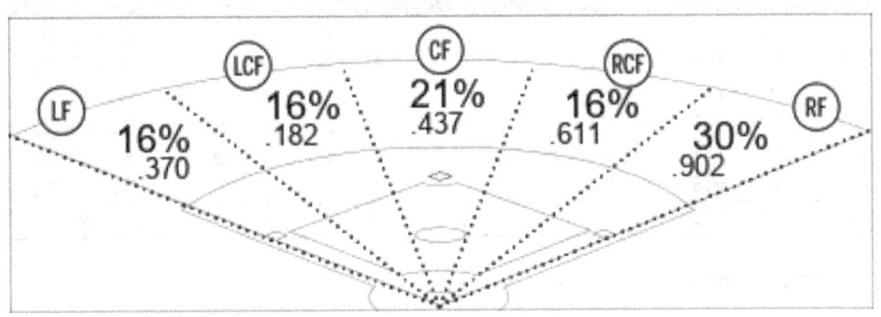

Strike Zone vs LHP   **Strike Zone vs RHP**

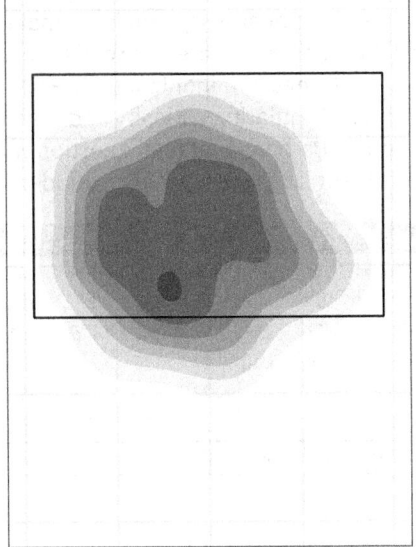

Cory Spangenberg UT

Born: 03/16/91   Age: 29   Bats: L   Throws: R
Height: 6'0"   Weight: 195   Origin: Round 1, 2011 Draft (#10 overall)

YEAR	TEAM	LVL	AGE	PA	R	2B	3B	HR	RBI	BB	K	SB	CS	AVG/OBP/SLG
2017	ELP	AAA	26	72	8	3	1	1	7	4	8	3	2	.348/.403/.470
2017	SDN	MLB	26	486	57	18	2	13	46	34	128	11	3	.264/.322/.401
2018	ELP	AAA	27	95	14	8	2	4	16	6	30	3	0	.341/.383/.614
2018	SDN	MLB	27	329	35	9	4	7	25	25	108	6	1	.235/.298/.362
2019	SAN	AAA	28	476	82	28	5	14	62	43	136	28	4	.309/.378/.498
2019	MIL	MLB	28	102	11	2	2	2	10	6	36	3	0	.232/.277/.358
2020	MIL	MLB	29	251	24	9	2	6	26	17	82	5	2	.237/.295/.372

Comparables: Randy Jackson, Jim Presley, Craig Paquette

Questions commonly asked when watching Spangenberg: "Wait, he's still around?" followed by "Wait, the G is soft?" Yes, Spangenberg still got occasional at-bats in 2019, and yes, it's pronounced "Spange" as in "Sponge." One other question he inspires, that also has an affirmative answer, is: "Can't they do better?" Spangenberg's ability to make consistent contact against big-league pitchers has evaporated. He can theoretically play multiple infield positions, but so can dozens of minor leaguers. Perhaps Spangenberg's best attribute at this point is stimulating curiosity and marvel. That counts for something, just not enough. Perhaps that final question will have a different answer on another continent, as the former first-rounder signed with the Seibu Lions for 2020.

YEAR	TEAM	LVL	AGE	PA	DRC+	VORP	BABIP	BRR	FRAA	WARP
2017	ELP	AAA	26	72	104	3.4	.386	-0.2	3B(17): -3.3	0.0
2017	SDN	MLB	26	486	82	28.5	.342	5.3	3B(96): -0.8, LF(32): -3.0	0.8
2018	ELP	AAA	27	95	116	6.4	.481	-0.4	3B(13): 0.8, 2B(5): -0.9	0.4
2018	SDN	MLB	27	329	64	4.6	.344	-0.1	2B(49): -2.8, 3B(44): 0.3	-0.7
2019	SAN	AAA	28	476	103	41.3	.422	5.6	LF(29): -2.6, 2B(20): -2.1	1.5
2019	MIL	MLB	28	102	47	-3.5	.351	-0.4	2B(22): 0.0, 3B(6): 0.4	-0.3
2020	MIL	MLB	29	251	75	0.8	.340	0.8	3B 1, 2B -1	0.0

Cory Spangenberg, continued

Batted Ball Distribution

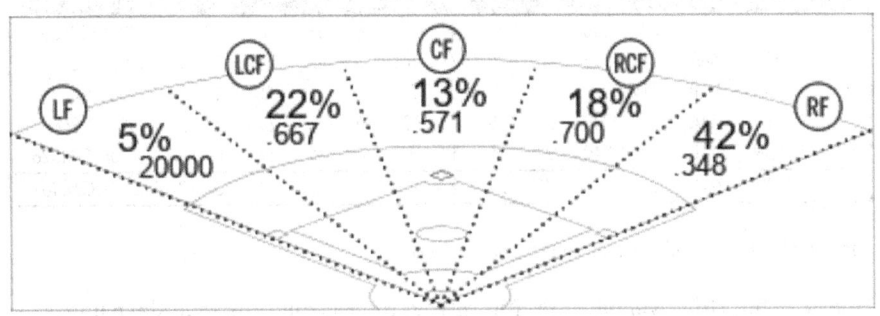

Strike Zone vs LHP   **Strike Zone vs RHP**

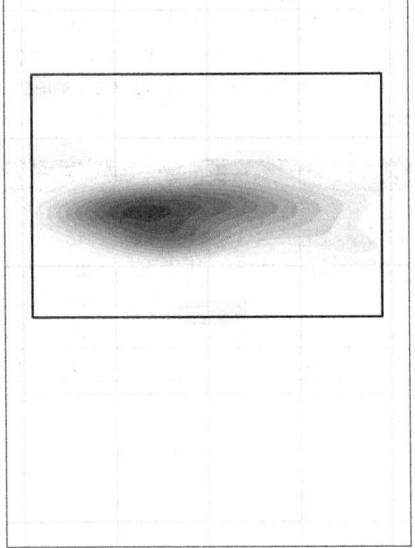

Luis Urías SS

Born: 06/03/97 Age: 23 Bats: R Throws: R
Height: 5'9" Weight: 185 Origin: International Free Agent, 2013

YEAR	TEAM	LVL	AGE	PA	R	2B	3B	HR	RBI	BB	K	SB	CS	AVG/OBP/SLG
2017	SAN	AA	20	526	77	20	4	3	38	68	65	7	5	.296/.398/.380
2018	ELP	AAA	21	533	83	30	7	8	45	67	109	2	1	.296/.398/.447
2018	SDN	MLB	21	53	5	1	0	2	5	3	10	1	0	.208/.264/.354
2019	ELP	AAA	22	339	62	19	4	19	50	36	62	7	2	.315/.398/.600
2019	SDN	MLB	22	249	27	8	1	4	24	25	56	0	1	.223/.329/.326
2020	MIL	MLB	23	455	49	21	2	12	51	42	91	3	2	.251/.336/.401

Comparables: Luis Rengifo, Wilmer Flores, Orlando Arcia

Urías can hit. Urías *will* hit. Urías has *always* hit. His minor-league slash line is .308/.397/.433. His Triple-A slash line is .305/.403/.511. Numbers like those sometimes comprise a lot of seasons for players who have been old for their level, or describe Quad-A corner men in the PCL. Urías will be *22 years old* on opening day, and he's a *middle infielder*. He spent his age 20 and 21 seasons in the high minors, during which he batted .296 and got on base at a .398 clip. The power may never come, he may not be an everyday shortstop and at the keystone he's more steady than spectacular. But Urías can hit. Trust us on this one.

YEAR	TEAM	LVL	AGE	PA	DRC+	VORP	BABIP	BRR	FRAA	WARP
2017	SAN	AA	20	526	132	42.3	.340	2.6	SS(60): 4.7, 2B(55): -1.1	4.2
2018	ELP	AAA	21	533	116	27.3	.373	1.4	2B(90): 10.2, SS(20): 3.4	4.5
2018	SDN	MLB	21	53	85	0.6	.216	0.3	2B(12): -0.2	0.1
2019	ELP	AAA	22	339	125	33.5	.343	2.5	SS(53): 8.5, 2B(21): 4.1	3.8
2019	SDN	MLB	22	249	83	5.1	.284	0.0	SS(41): -5.4, 2B(26): -1.7	-0.2
2020	MIL	MLB	23	455	98	16.4	.297	0.2	SS 2, 2B 0	2.0

Luis Urías, continued

Batted Ball Distribution

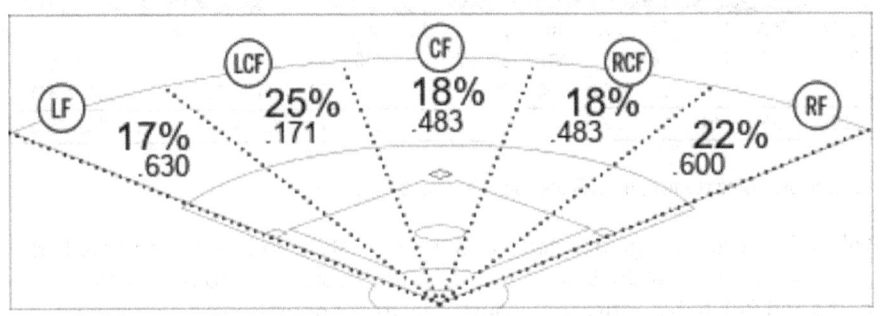

Strike Zone vs LHP   **Strike Zone vs RHP**

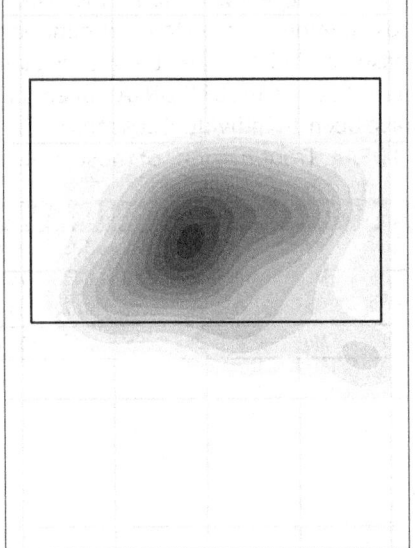

Christian Yelich RF

Born: 12/05/91   Age: 28   Bats: L   Throws: R
Height: 6'3"   Weight: 195   Origin: Round 1, 2010 Draft (#23 overall)

YEAR	TEAM	LVL	AGE	PA	R	2B	3B	HR	RBI	BB	K	SB	CS	AVG/OBP/SLG
2017	MIA	MLB	25	695	100	36	2	18	81	80	137	16	2	.282/.369/.439
2018	MIL	MLB	26	651	118	34	7	36	110	68	135	22	4	.326/.402/.598
2019	MIL	MLB	27	580	100	29	3	44	97	80	118	30	2	.329/.429/.671
2020	MIL	MLB	28	595	91	26	2	36	101	73	129	14	4	.295/.387/.563

Comparables: Greg Luzinski, Travis Snider, Stephen Piscotty

Milwaukee's glorious golden god, Yelich took his MVP 2018 season and made it better in every way in 2019; from surface counting stats like homers, stolen bases and RBI, to his entire triple-slash line, to peripherals like walk rate and isolated power. He's improved from a well-rounded hitter with the Marlins to elite in every facet of the game for the Brewers thanks to swing adjustments and an impeccable feel for hard contact—he finished fifth in exit velocity, behind a bunch of players who "look" more like sluggers. He has, essentially, become the closest thing we have to a left-handed Mike Trout. Despite the fact that Yelich's season ended with just 130 games played after he fouled a ball off his kneecap in September, his 53.4 DRAA trailed only Alex Bregman and, well, Trout. There have been 14 individual seasons in the past five years where a batter has topped 50 DRAA. Trout has four of those; Yelich will look for his second in 2020.

YEAR	TEAM	LVL	AGE	PA	DRC+	VORP	BABIP	BRR	FRAA	WARP
2017	MIA	MLB	25	695	105	45.6	.336	0.8	CF(155): -17.3	1.2
2018	MIL	MLB	26	651	143	79.0	.373	2.4	LF(90): -7.3, RF(75): 2.1	4.8
2019	MIL	MLB	27	580	167	64.4	.355	3.7	RF(124): -1.6, LF(6): 0.5	6.5
2020	MIL	MLB	28	595	149	51.1	.330	0.4	RF -1	5.2

Christian Yelich, continued

Batted Ball Distribution

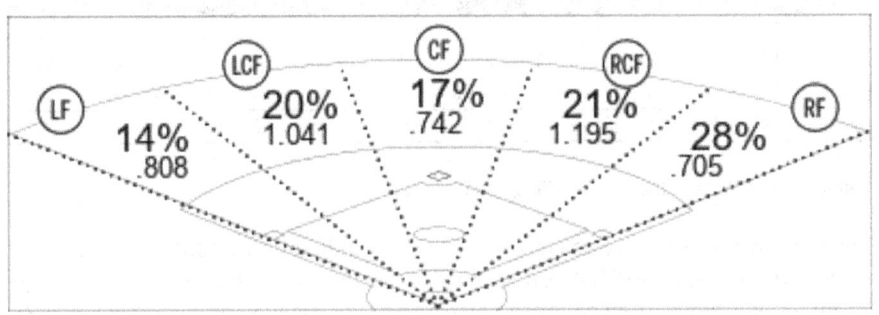

Strike Zone vs LHP   **Strike Zone vs RHP**

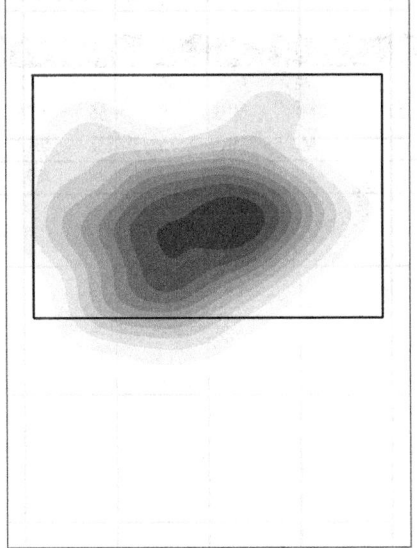

Matt Albers RHP

Born: 01/20/83 Age: 37 Bats: L Throws: R
Height: 6'1" Weight: 225 Origin: Round 23, 2001 Draft (#686 overall)

YEAR	TEAM	LVL	AGE	W	L	SV	G	GS	IP	H	HR	BB/9	K/9	K	GB%	BABIP
2017	WAS	MLB	34	7	2	2	63	0	61	35	6	2.5	9.3	63	52%	.203
2018	MIL	MLB	35	3	3	1	34	0	34[1]	45	10	3.1	8.4	32	47%	.347
2019	MIL	MLB	36	8	6	4	67	0	59[2]	53	8	4.4	8.6	57	52%	.280
2020	MIL	MLB	37	2	2	0	33	0	35	36	5	3.8	8.3	32	50%	.301

Comparables: David Weathers, Mike Fetters, Bob Wickman

For a second consecutive season, it was a story of first half versus second half. Albers struck out 38 and held opponents to a .216/.282/.358 batting line through 37 first-half innings, then collapsed after the break. He walked 18 batters in 22 ⅔ second-half innings and allowed a .402 on-base percentage. That was essentially the same story as 2018, when Albers was solid through the first half and was awful down the stretch. Albers will turn 37 years old in 2020. Another year probably won't help him retain a full season's worth of gas.

YEAR	TEAM	LVL	AGE	WHIP	ERA	DRA	WARP	MPH	FB%	WHF	CSP
2017	WAS	MLB	34	0.85	1.62	3.93	0.8	95.6	67.7	10.1	49.5
2018	MIL	MLB	35	1.66	7.34	6.09	-0.5	94.5	64.6	11.6	44.1
2019	MIL	MLB	36	1.37	5.13	4.79	0.4	95.0	56.7	10.1	40.7
2020	MIL	MLB	37	1.44	4.92	4.83	0.2	93.6	60.2	10.2	43

Matt Albers, continued

Pitch Shape vs LHH

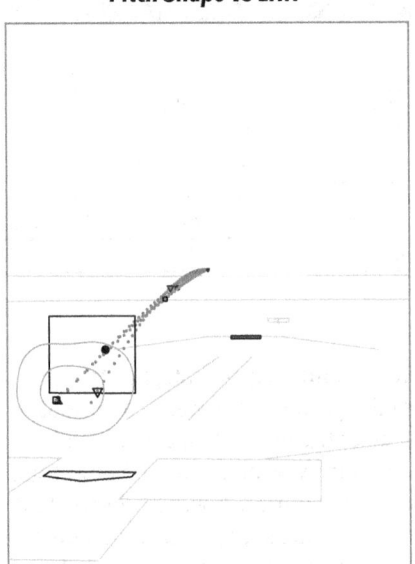

Pitch Shape vs RHH

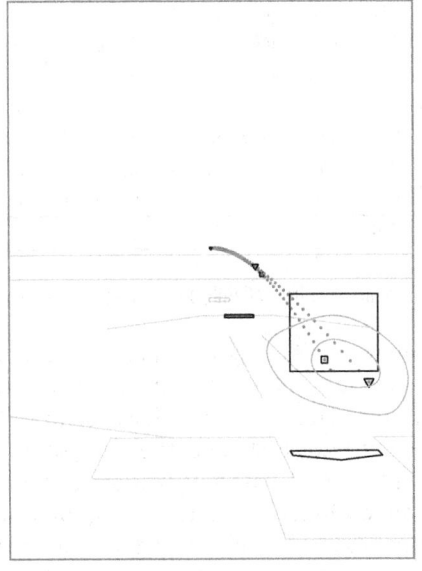

Type	Frequency	Velocity	H Movement	V Movement
● Fastball	10.3%	93.6 [103]	-11.1 [81]	-17 [97]
□ Sinker	46.4%	93.1 [102]	-15.2 [84]	-22.6 [92]
+ Cutter				
▲ Changeup	10.2%	84 [96]	-12.3 [95]	-30.8 [90]
× Splitter				
▽ Slider	32.9%	83.8 [97]	5.3 [101]	-34 [97]
◇ Curveball				
⊕ Slow Curveball				
✳ Knuckleball				
▼ Screwball				

Brewers Player Analysis - 53

Brett Anderson LHP

Born: 02/01/88 Age: 32 Bats: L Throws: L
Height: 6'4" Weight: 230 Origin: Round 2, 2006 Draft (#55 overall)

YEAR	TEAM	LVL	AGE	W	L	SV	G	GS	IP	H	HR	BB/9	K/9	K	GB%	BABIP
2017	TEN	AA	29	2	2	0	6	5	27^1	34	2	3.0	4.9	15	69%	.348
2017	BUF	AAA	29	1	1	0	2	2	9^2	4	0	1.9	2.8	3	53%	.133
2017	CHN	MLB	29	2	2	0	6	6	22	34	2	4.9	6.5	16	51%	.395
2017	TOR	MLB	29	2	2	0	7	7	33^1	39	3	2.4	5.9	22	50%	.340
2018	NAS	AAA	30	2	1	0	7	7	32^1	32	0	1.7	10.0	36	60%	.333
2018	OAK	MLB	30	4	5	0	17	17	80^1	90	10	1.5	5.3	47	57%	.307
2019	OAK	MLB	31	13	9	0	31	31	176	181	20	2.5	4.6	90	56%	.278
2020	MIL	MLB	32	8	8	0	23	23	129	145	19	2.5	5.1	74	56%	.295

Comparables: Trevor Cahill, John Danks, Jaime García

There aren't many starters who can survive without missing bats, but together Anderson and the A's found a formula. His elite ground ball rate, a cavernous yard and tremendous defense on the left side of the infield helped Oakland wring a 3.89 ERA out of the aging southpaw, which was nearly a run better than his DRA. And what a delightfully unexpected contribution it was: Anderson had topped 20 starts and 120 innings only once all decade so, sure, why wouldn't he fire 175 frames for a playoff team in the September of his career? The lefty's surprising durability was a shot in the arm for a staff otherwise battered by injuries and suspensions all year long. It's unlikely he gives them 30 starts, but the Brewers, perennially short on starters, inked him to a one-year deal in December.

YEAR	TEAM	LVL	AGE	WHIP	ERA	DRA	WARP	MPH	FB%	WHF	CSP
2017	TEN	AA	29	1.57	4.61	6.45	-0.4				
2017	BUF	AAA	29	0.62	0.93	2.37	0.4				
2017	CHN	MLB	29	2.09	8.18	4.87	0.2	92.5	56.7	9	41.6
2017	TOR	MLB	29	1.44	5.13	5.88	-0.1	93.4	48.6	9.5	46.3
2018	NAS	AAA	30	1.18	2.78	3.21	0.9				
2018	OAK	MLB	30	1.28	4.48	3.98	1.2	93.1	49.5	8.1	49.2
2019	OAK	MLB	31	1.31	3.89	5.65	0.2	93.4	49.7	8.1	51.7
2020	MIL	MLB	32	1.40	4.89	4.97	1.2	92.4	49.5	8.2	48.5

Brett Anderson, continued

Pitch Shape vs LHH

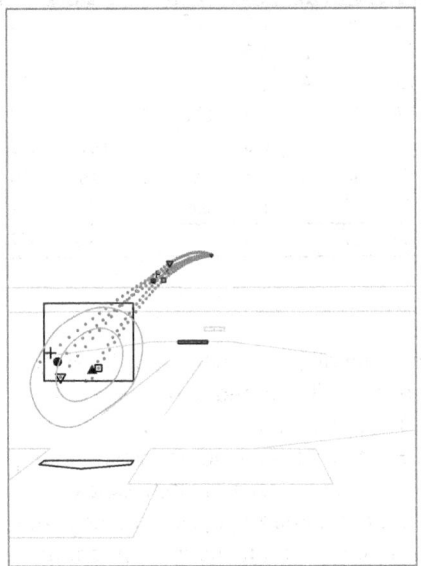

Pitch Shape vs RHH

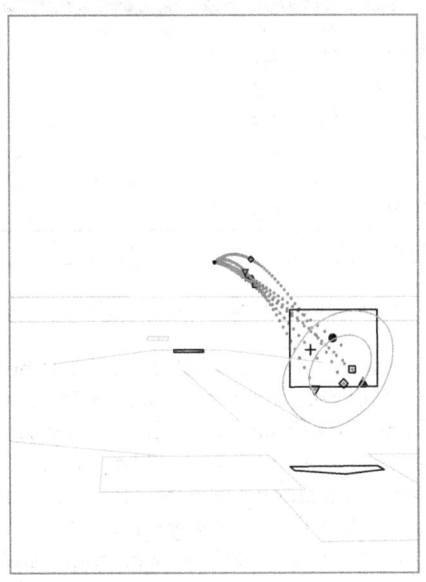

Type	Frequency	Velocity	H Movement	V Movement
● Fastball	6.7%	91.5 [97]	7.2 [99]	-17.1 [97]
□ Sinker	42.9%	91 [92]	13.4 [95]	-22.6 [92]
+ Cutter	12.5%	88.9 [101]	1.5 [81]	-21.6 [109]
▲ Changeup	13.5%	82.9 [91]	12.7 [93]	-29.7 [93]
✕ Splitter				
▽ Slider	18.7%	82.2 [91]	-3.5 [94]	-43.2 [71]
◇ Curveball	5.6%	76 [91]	-5.8 [93]	-56.3 [82]
✦ Slow Curveball				
✳ Knuckleball				
▼ Screwball				

Ray Black   RHP

Born: 06/26/90   Age: 30   Bats: R   Throws: R
Height: 6'5"   Weight: 225   Origin: Round 7, 2011 Draft (#237 overall)

YEAR	TEAM	LVL	AGE	W	L	SV	G	GS	IP	H	HR	BB/9	K/9	K	GB%	BABIP
2018	RIC	AA	28	0	0	4	10	0	10	4	0	3.6	18.0	20	7%	.286
2018	SAC	AAA	28	3	0	1	26	0	25^2	15	2	2.8	16.1	46	25%	.310
2018	SFN	MLB	28	2	2	0	26	0	23^1	17	4	3.9	12.7	33	41%	.277
2019	SAC	AAA	29	1	0	1	23	1	22^2	19	4	5.2	14.3	36	38%	.349
2019	SAN	AAA	29	0	0	1	6	0	6	1	0	3.0	13.5	9	60%	.100
2019	SFN	MLB	29	0	0	0	2	0	2	4	1	4.5	22.5	5	0%	.750
2019	MIL	MLB	29	0	1	0	15	0	14	10	4	5.1	8.4	13	30%	.182
2020	MIL	MLB	30	3	3	0	56	0	60	51	10	4.3	12.5	83	33%	.309

Comparables: Grant Dayton, Robert Coello, Leonel Campos

In a sense, it's remarkable Black has been a functional pitcher at any level, given that his only real tool is a fastball he locates as well and frequently as blindfolded children do the donkey's tail. That's the value—or allure, anyway—of velocity. He averaged 98.4 MPH on his fourseamer in 2019, ranking him ninth among relievers who threw at least one big-league pitch. Black was even ahead of some guy named Aroldis Chapman. Imagining what Black could do with marginally improved command is a fool's errand, but every pitching coach needs hope in their life, even if it proves to be misplaced—like, um, a certain right-hander's heater.

YEAR	TEAM	LVL	AGE	WHIP	ERA	DRA	WARP	MPH	FB%	WHF	CSP
2018	RIC	AA	28	0.80	0.90	1.54	0.4				
2018	SAC	AAA	28	0.90	3.16	1.79	1.0				
2018	SFN	MLB	28	1.16	6.17	2.66	0.6	100.5	64	17.1	45.7
2019	SAC	AAA	29	1.41	5.16	3.72	0.6				
2019	SAN	AAA	29	0.50	1.50	5.93	0.0				
2019	SFN	MLB	29	2.50	4.50	3.61	0.0	101.5	71.2	17.3	57.1
2019	MIL	MLB	29	1.29	5.14	7.42	-0.3	99.8	76.3	13.7	46.6
2020	MIL	MLB	30	1.34	4.26	4.25	0.8	99.5	68.9	15.9	47.2

Ray Black, continued

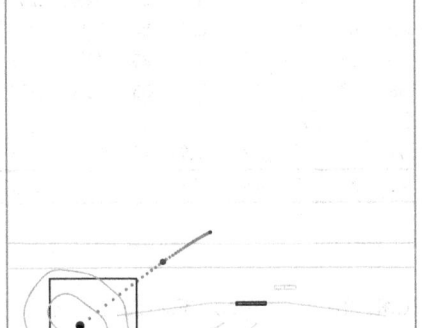

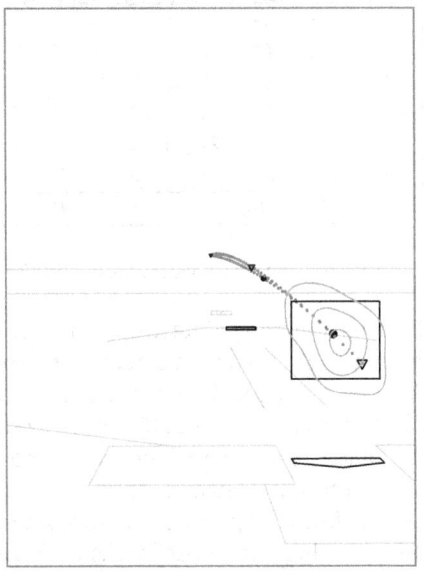

Type	Frequency	Velocity	H Movement	V Movement
● Fastball	75.3%	98.4 [117]	-7.1 [99]	-11.7 [111]
☐ Sinker				
+ Cutter				
▲ Changeup				
✕ Splitter				
▽ Slider	24.7%	86.2 [108]	9.7 [120]	-33 [100]
◇ Curveball				
⊕ Slow Curveball				
✳ Knuckleball				
▼ Screwball				

Corbin Burnes   RHP

Born: 10/22/94   Age: 25   Bats: R   Throws: R
Height: 6'3"   Weight: 205   Origin: Round 4, 2016 Draft (#111 overall)

YEAR	TEAM	LVL	AGE	W	L	SV	G	GS	IP	H	HR	BB/9	K/9	K	GB%	BABIP
2017	CAR	A+	22	5	0	0	10	10	60	37	1	2.4	8.4	56	54%	.243
2017	BLX	AA	22	3	3	0	16	16	85^2	66	2	2.1	8.8	84	51%	.279
2018	CSP	AAA	23	3	4	0	19	13	78^2	83	7	3.5	9.3	81	47%	.347
2018	MIL	MLB	23	7	0	1	30	0	38	27	4	2.6	8.3	35	50%	.232
2019	SAN	AAA	24	0	1	0	8	7	22^1	29	2	3.6	10.1	25	50%	.409
2019	MIL	MLB	24	1	5	1	32	4	49	70	17	3.7	12.9	70	46%	.414
2020	MIL	MLB	25	4	4	0	46	6	74	66	10	3.9	11.8	97	47%	.317

Comparables: John Gant, Cody Martin, Hunter Wood

Disaster. Calamity. Catastrophe. Debacle. Cataclysm. Tragedy. Fiasco. We're running out of synonyms here, but all of them perfectly describe Burnes' 2019. After giving up just four homers in 38 frames in 2018, batters teed off for 17 blasts in 48 innings in 2019—that's a ridiculous 3.1 per nine, for those without a calculator handy. His slider was still nasty, as it finished off a majority of his strikeouts, but he just couldn't get the fastball by hitters. That's a notable change from the previous season, when he held opponents to a .176 average and .250 slugging (those marks were up to .420 and .790 last season). The Brewers have to hope some time to reflect can help Burnes get back on track as a mid-rotation starter.

YEAR	TEAM	LVL	AGE	WHIP	ERA	DRA	WARP	MPH	FB%	WHF	CSP
2017	CAR	A+	22	0.88	1.05	2.37	2.0				
2017	BLX	AA	22	1.00	2.10	3.23	2.0				
2018	CSP	AAA	23	1.45	5.15	4.30	1.1				
2018	MIL	MLB	23	1.00	2.61	3.39	0.7	97.6	58.8	15.8	50.6
2019	SAN	AAA	24	1.70	8.46	3.70	0.6				
2019	MIL	MLB	24	1.84	8.82	4.99	0.3	98.0	56.8	18	45.7
2020	MIL	MLB	25	1.32	4.09	4.12	1.2	97.6	58.9	17.7	49.1

Corbin Burnes, continued

Pitch Shape vs LHH

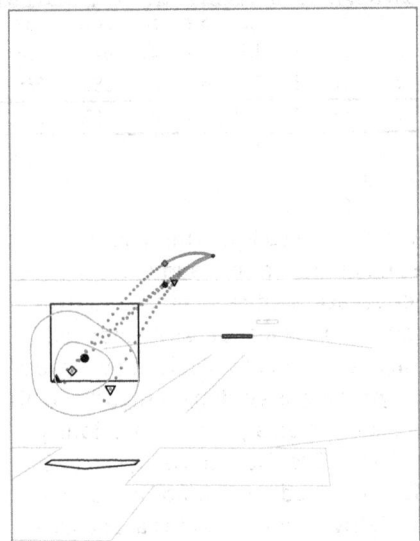

Pitch Shape vs RHH

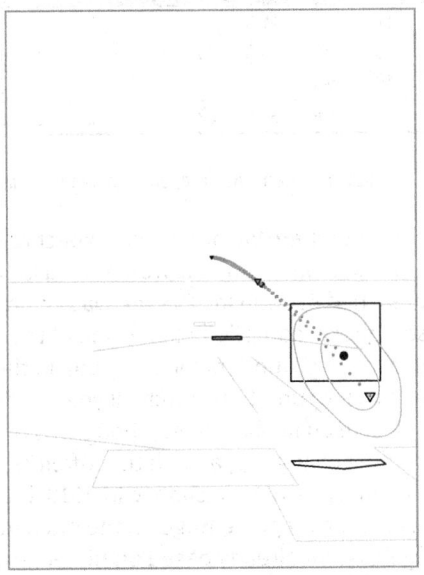

Type	Frequency	Velocity	H Movement	V Movement
● Fastball	53.6%	95.6 [109]	-1.4 [124]	-14.6 [103]
☐ Sinker	3.3%	96 [118]	-11.1 [110]	-15.6 [117]
+ Cutter				
▲ Changeup	3.9%	91.2 [122]	-9.8 [106]	-24 [110]
✕ Splitter				
▽ Slider	31.1%	88.3 [117]	5.9 [104]	-30.2 [108]
◇ Curveball	8.1%	81.7 [110]	10.5 [112]	-42 [112]
⊕ Slow Curveball				
✳ Knuckleball				
▼ Screwball				

Alex Claudio LHP

Born: 01/31/92 Age: 28 Bats: L Throws: L
Height: 6'3" Weight: 180 Origin: Round 27, 2010 Draft (#826 overall)

YEAR	TEAM	LVL	AGE	W	L	SV	G	GS	IP	H	HR	BB/9	K/9	K	GB%	BABIP
2017	TEX	MLB	25	4	2	11	70	1	82^2	71	5	1.6	6.1	56	68%	.269
2018	TEX	MLB	26	4	2	1	66	1	68^1	91	4	1.7	5.4	41	64%	.366
2019	MIL	MLB	27	2	2	0	83	0	62	57	8	3.5	6.4	44	58%	.266
2020	MIL	MLB	28	3	3	2	56	0	60	55	7	2.6	6.5	43	60%	.269

Comparables: Jeremy Accardo, Brandon Maurer, Cla Meredith

In times where we practically expect relievers to bring 95-plus mph heat, Claudio feels like a relic from the past. Despite the fact that Claudio never once breached 89 mph in 2019, he was an above-replacement reliever for a fourth-straight season. His sinker is one of the heaviest in the league, as he induced nearly 2.5 grounders for every ball in the air, and he did that while allowing just one home run off the pitch all year. Not everything was golden for Claudio in his first season in Milwaukee, though, as hitters connected against his previously baffling changeup, a pitch that often clocks in the 60s. After allowing just a .296 slugging against the change in 2018, hitters connected for four homers and a .471 slugging percentage on the pitch in 2019. Given how the odds are stacked against him already based on his well-below-average velocity, he'll need to correct that in 2020 if he's to have a 2021.

YEAR	TEAM	LVL	AGE	WHIP	ERA	DRA	WARP	MPH	FB%	WHF	CSP
2017	TEX	MLB	25	1.04	2.50	3.77	1.3	88.4	56.6	10.6	45.8
2018	TEX	MLB	26	1.52	4.48	4.69	0.2	88.1	52	12.3	45.1
2019	MIL	MLB	27	1.31	4.06	4.93	0.3	87.6	46.2	11.3	41.1
2020	MIL	MLB	28	1.21	3.64	3.83	1.0	87.5	51.3	11.5	43.9

Alex Claudio, continued

Pitch Shape vs LHH

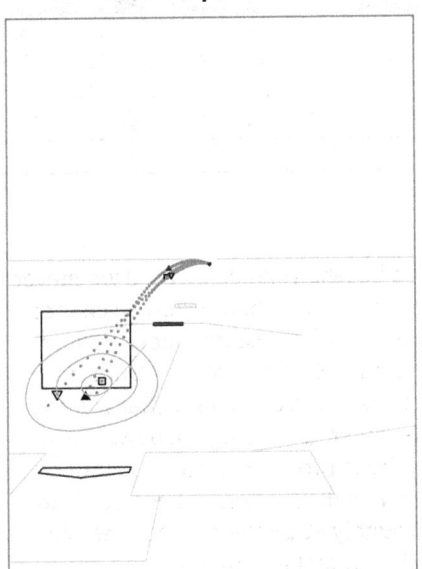

Pitch Shape vs RHH

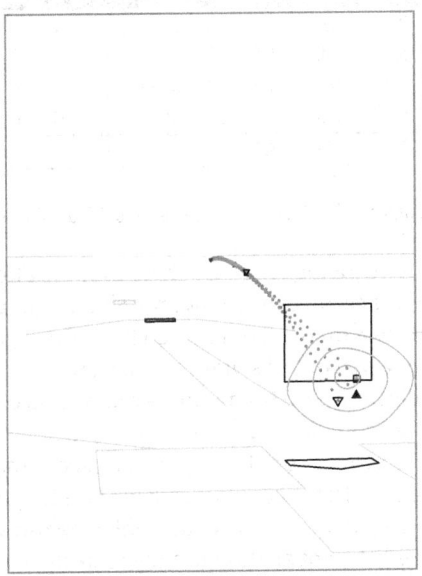

Type	Frequency	Velocity	H Movement	V Movement
● Fastball				
☐ Sinker	46.2%	85.9 [65]	15.6 [81]	-37.4 [40]
+ Cutter				
▲ Changeup	36.2%	73.6 [58]	18 [68]	-46.3 [45]
✕ Splitter				
▽ Slider	17.7%	76.8 [68]	-4.9 [100]	-39.3 [82]
◇ Curveball				
⊕ Slow Curveball				
✱ Knuckleball				
▼ Screwball				

Josh Hader LHP

Born: 04/07/94 Age: 26 Bats: L Throws: L
Height: 6'3" Weight: 185 Origin: Round 19, 2012 Draft (#582 overall)

YEAR	TEAM	LVL	AGE	W	L	SV	G	GS	IP	H	HR	BB/9	K/9	K	GB%	BABIP
2017	CSP	AAA	23	3	4	0	12	12	52	49	14	5.4	8.8	51	37%	.265
2017	MIL	MLB	23	2	3	0	35	0	47^2	25	4	4.2	12.8	68	36%	.233
2018	MIL	MLB	24	6	1	12	55	0	81^1	36	9	3.3	15.8	143	31%	.220
2019	MIL	MLB	25	3	5	37	61	0	75^2	41	15	2.4	16.4	138	22%	.232
2020	MIL	MLB	26	3	3	36	62	0	66	41	10	3.6	16.5	120	29%	.300

Comparables: Stephen Gonsalves, Touki Toussaint, Justus Sheffield

We're joking when we write that the altered baseball should be used whenever Hader is on the mound, but that might be the only way batters have a chance. Hitters made contact even less often against Hader last season, down to just 58.2 percent of swings (versus 60.5 percent in 2018). Yet 15 of the 41 hits he allowed were home runs—that works out to 21.4 percent of his flyballs. Woof. We can talk all we want about pitchers like Hader "providing the power" with the velocity on their fastballs, except that's been proven to be an overstated factor. The bigger factor, if we had to guess, was that batters are geared up to swing hard on his heater, which he threw roughly 80 percent of the time. May as well; it's not as though they're likely to make contact regardless.

YEAR	TEAM	LVL	AGE	WHIP	ERA	DRA	WARP	MPH	FB%	WHF	CSP
2017	CSP	AAA	23	1.54	5.37	4.82	0.5				
2017	MIL	MLB	23	0.99	2.08	3.31	1.0	97.1	81.4	18.4	49.4
2018	MIL	MLB	24	0.81	2.43	2.00	2.7	97.4	79.1	20.5	51.7
2019	MIL	MLB	25	0.81	2.62	2.20	2.6	97.9	84.1	24.4	51
2020	MIL	MLB	26	1.03	2.68	2.85	1.8	97.2	83.1	22.2	51.8

Josh Hader, continued

	Pitch Shape vs LHH	Pitch Shape vs RHH
	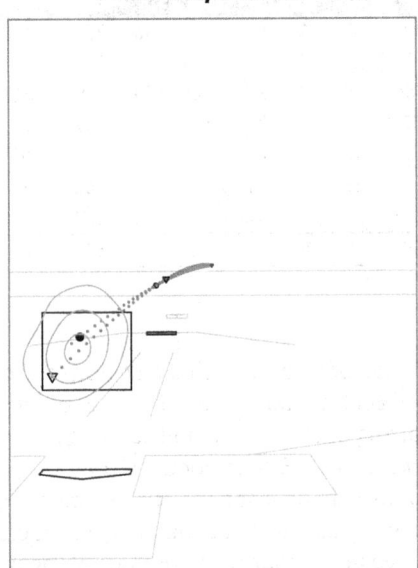	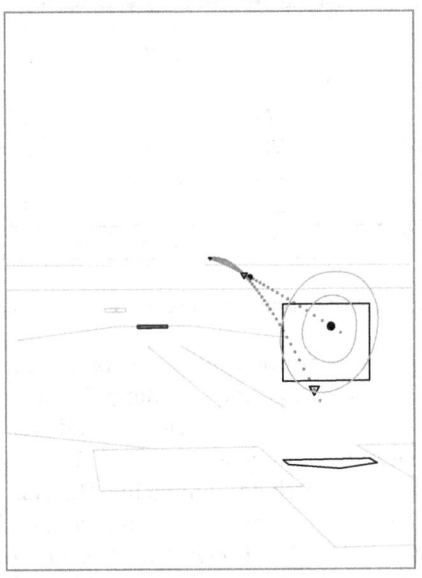

Type	Frequency	Velocity	H Movement	V Movement
● Fastball	84.1%	95.9 [110]	8.9 [91]	-11.2 [112]
☐ Sinker				
+ Cutter				
▲ Changeup				
× Splitter				
▽ Slider	15.5%	82.1 [90]	-6.2 [105]	-34.2 [97]
◇ Curveball				
⊕ Slow Curveball				
✳ Knuckleball				
▼ Screwball				

Adrian Houser   RHP

Born: 02/02/93   Age: 27   Bats: R   Throws: R
Height: 6'4"   Weight: 235   Origin: Round 2, 2011 Draft (#69 overall)

YEAR	TEAM	LVL	AGE	W	L	SV	G	GS	IP	H	HR	BB/9	K/9	K	GB%	BABIP
2017	BRR	RK	24	0	1	0	6	6	8.2	4	1	4.2	16.6	16	73%	.214
2017	WIS	A	24	1	0	0	3	2	9	5	0	0.0	11.0	11	71%	.238
2018	BLX	AA	25	0	1	0	8	8	26.2	30	3	2.4	10.1	30	51%	.365
2018	CSP	AAA	25	2	3	0	13	13	52	66	6	3.1	6.4	37	54%	.357
2018	MIL	MLB	25	0	0	0	7	0	13.2	13	0	4.6	5.3	8	40%	.302
2019	SAN	AAA	26	2	0	0	4	4	21.1	13	2	1.7	9.7	23	56%	.212
2019	MIL	MLB	26	6	7	0	35	18	111.1	101	14	3.0	9.5	117	55%	.301
2020	MIL	MLB	27	8	8	0	26	26	122	117	16	3.3	9.2	124	54%	.305

Comparables: Jarlin García, Rookie Davis, Steven Shell

Believe it or not, Houser was part of the Carlos Gómez trade that also netted the Brewers Josh Hader, Domingo Santana and Brett Phillips. (Hey, three out of four ain't bad.) Houser showed aptitude for starting in the second half, fanning a batter per inning over his final 77 innings with a 4.02 ERA to boot. A strong offspeed pitch has eluded him thus far, but he's doing just fine with a 95 mph four-seamer that can leap over bats and a heavy sinker that generates grounders as need be. The Brewers will presumably give him a chance to continue along in the rotation. Worst-case: he can transition back into the multi-inning relief role that he was quite good in earlier in the season.

YEAR	TEAM	LVL	AGE	WHIP	ERA	DRA	WARP	MPH	FB%	WHF	CSP
2017	BRR	RK	24	0.92	1.04	0.00	0.6				
2017	WIS	A	24	0.56	1.00	2.11	0.3				
2018	BLX	AA	25	1.39	4.72	6.34	-0.3				
2018	CSP	AAA	25	1.62	5.19	5.89	-0.2				
2018	MIL	MLB	25	1.46	3.29	5.04	0.0	96.7	66.4	11.1	44.7
2019	SAN	AAA	26	0.80	1.27	1.39	1.1				
2019	MIL	MLB	26	1.24	3.72	3.61	2.5	96.4	67.4	10.5	47.2
2020	MIL	MLB	27	1.33	4.27	4.32	2.0	95.9	68.1	10.7	46.6

Adrian Houser, continued

Pitch Shape vs LHH

Pitch Shape vs RHH

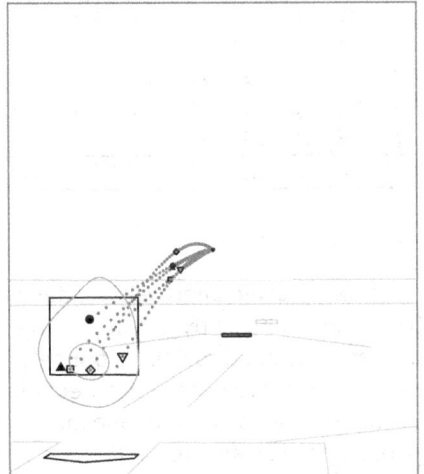
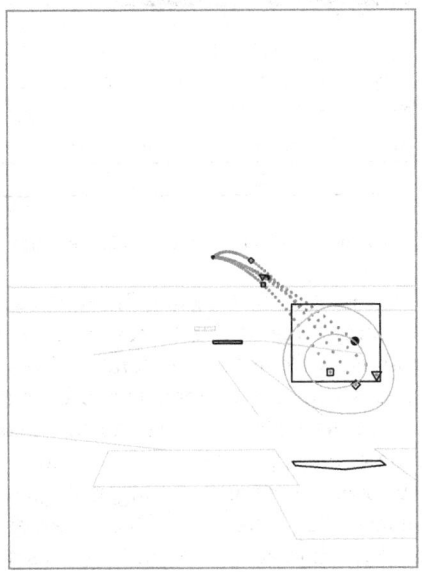

Type	Frequency	Velocity	H Movement	V Movement
● Fastball	31.3%	94.9 [107]	-5.8 [105]	-13.8 [106]
☐ Sinker	36.0%	94.6 [110]	-13 [98]	-20 [101]
+ Cutter				
▲ Changeup	7.0%	85.7 [102]	-11.3 [99]	-28.6 [96]
✕ Splitter				
▽ Slider	11.7%	88.2 [116]	3.9 [95]	-26.6 [119]
◇ Curveball	13.9%	80.8 [107]	3.1 [82]	-51.3 [92]
⊕ Slow Curveball				
✲ Knuckleball				
▼ Screwball				

Milwaukee Brewers 2020

Eric Lauer LHP

Born: 06/03/95   Age: 25   Bats: R   Throws: L
Height: 6'3"   Weight: 205   Origin: Round 1, 2016 Draft (#25 overall)

YEAR	TEAM	LVL	AGE	W	L	SV	G	GS	IP	H	HR	BB/9	K/9	K	GB%	BABIP
2017	LEL	A+	22	2	5	0	12	12	67^2	65	4	2.5	11.2	84	42%	.351
2017	SAN	AA	22	4	3	0	10	9	55	52	6	2.8	7.9	48	38%	.295
2018	ELP	AAA	23	2	1	0	4	4	21^1	13	1	3.8	9.3	22	48%	.226
2018	SDN	MLB	23	6	7	0	23	23	112	127	15	3.7	8.0	100	39%	.332
2019	SDN	MLB	24	8	10	0	30	29	149^2	158	20	3.1	8.3	138	42%	.316
2020	MIL	MLB	25	9	9	0	26	26	137	140	22	3.0	7.9	121	41%	.297

Comparables: Antonio Bastardo, David Price, Derek Holland

Lauer earned the Opening Day nod last spring and showed improvement during his second year in the Padres rotation, pitching more efficiently and improving both his walk and strikeout rates. The young lefty doesn't throw hard, but he's always around the zone and shows solid command, with a wide assortment of curveballs, sliders, cutters and changeups. That mix helps his mundane four-seamer play up and keep him effective against righties. Lauer doesn't have a true swing-and-miss offering, isn't going to toss any shutouts and won't be a top jersey-seller. Instead, he'll hit his target, control the running game, post average numbers and keep his team in games more often than not, from a spot at the back of the rotation. That's a lot more valuable than most people think.

YEAR	TEAM	LVL	AGE	WHIP	ERA	DRA	WARP	MPH	FB%	WHF	CSP
2017	LEL	A+	22	1.24	2.79	3.93	1.1				
2017	SAN	AA	22	1.25	3.93	4.77	0.2				
2018	ELP	AAA	23	1.03	2.53	2.76	0.7				
2018	SDN	MLB	23	1.54	4.34	5.27	0.1	94.0	57.8	9.7	51.5
2019	SDN	MLB	24	1.40	4.45	4.85	1.5	94.0	53	9.5	51.5
2020	MIL	MLB	25	1.35	4.60	4.66	1.8	93.7	56.1	9.8	52.7

Eric Lauer, continued

Pitch Shape vs LHH

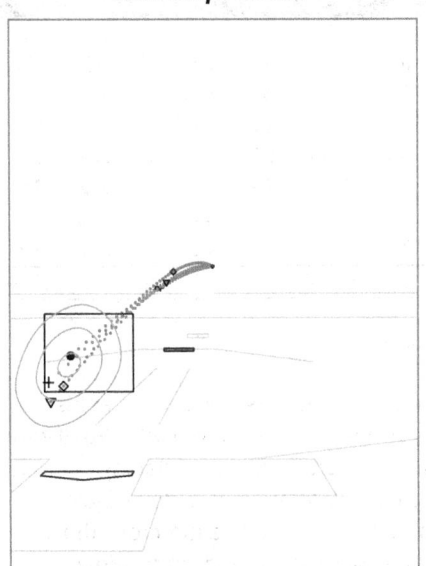

Pitch Shape vs RHH

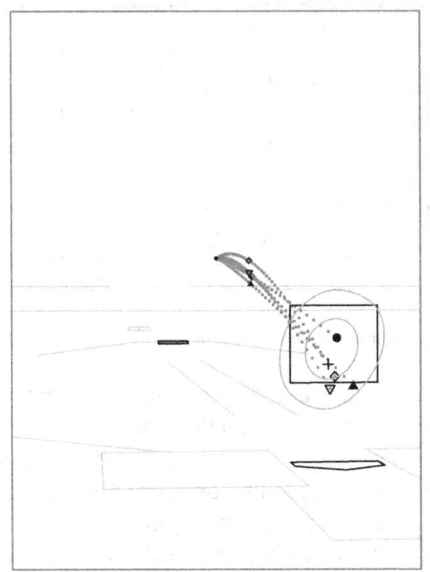

Type	Frequency	Velocity	H Movement	V Movement
● Fastball	53.0%	92.1 [99]	8.6 [92]	-13.9 [105]
☐ Sinker				
+ Cutter	21.7%	88.2 [97]	-0.9 [95]	-23 [104]
▲ Changeup	3.7%	86.2 [103]	12.3 [95]	-21.8 [117]
✕ Splitter				
▽ Slider	4.2%	82.7 [93]	-1.5 [85]	-36.2 [91]
◇ Curveball	17.4%	77.9 [98]	-3.2 [83]	-45.7 [104]
⊕ Slow Curveball				
✱ Knuckleball				
▼ Screwball				

Mike Morin   RHP

Born: 05/03/91   Age: 29   Bats: R   Throws: R
Height: 6'4"   Weight: 220   Origin: Round 13, 2012 Draft (#417 overall)

YEAR	TEAM	LVL	AGE	W	L	SV	G	GS	IP	H	HR	BB/9	K/9	K	GB%	BABIP
2017	SLC	AAA	26	0	1	1	22	1	39.1	34	5	1.6	5.7	25	34%	.252
2017	LAA	MLB	26	0	0	0	10	0	14.1	21	3	1.3	6.3	10	54%	.367
2017	KCA	MLB	26	0	0	0	6	0	5.2	8	0	4.8	9.5	6	42%	.421
2018	TAC	AAA	27	5	2	3	41	3	53.2	51	3	2.2	8.7	52	43%	.308
2018	SEA	MLB	27	0	0	0	3	0	4	6	0	2.2	13.5	6	27%	.545
2019	ROC	AAA	28	0	1	1	8	1	12	11	1	2.2	9.0	12	37%	.294
2019	MIN	MLB	28	0	0	1	23	0	22.2	20	3	0.8	4.4	11	48%	.230
2019	PHI	MLB	28	1	3	0	29	0	28	26	3	2.6	4.8	15	37%	.256
2020	PHI	MLB	29	2	2	0	33	0	35	34	6	2.4	7.3	28	43%	.276

Comparables: Kelvin Herrera, Kevin Jepsen, Tom Niedenfuer

It was logical to believe Morin's brief tenure in the majors was over after his excellent changeup disappeared three years ago, but he resurfaced in 2019 with the Twins before trading places with cash considerations and surfacing in Philly. Everything about Morin, from the lack of a quality offering outside of that cambio to an apparent pitch-to-contact strategy that led to a ludicrous dip in strikeouts, defied any kind of expectations. A mediocre ERA despite a low batting average against suggests Morin was unlucky but his DRA indicates Morin should have been tagged even harder by opposing batters. Relief arms can resurface at any given moment, so this is either the last time you'll read about Morin in this space or he'll find his way into the next 20 *Baseball Prospectus* annuals.

YEAR	TEAM	LVL	AGE	WHIP	ERA	DRA	WARP	MPH	FB%	WHF	CSP
2017	SLC	AAA	26	1.04	3.20	3.29	0.9				
2017	LAA	MLB	26	1.60	6.91	2.88	0.4	93.0	47.3	13.7	43.3
2017	KCA	MLB	26	1.94	7.94	4.32	0.1	91.9	47.3	14.6	49.5
2018	TAC	AAA	27	1.19	3.86	3.62	1.0				
2018	SEA	MLB	27	1.75	6.75	7.63	-0.1	93.0	41.5	13.9	52.1
2019	ROC	AAA	28	1.17	2.25	3.40	0.3				
2019	MIN	MLB	28	0.97	3.18	6.34	-0.2	93.4	49.1	12.6	53.1
2019	PHI	MLB	28	1.21	5.79	5.50	0.0	93.0	46.9	10.9	45.9
2020	PHI	MLB	29	1.24	4.17	4.37	0.4	92.4	47.4	12.2	49

Mike Morin, continued

Pitch Shape vs LHH	Pitch Shape vs RHH
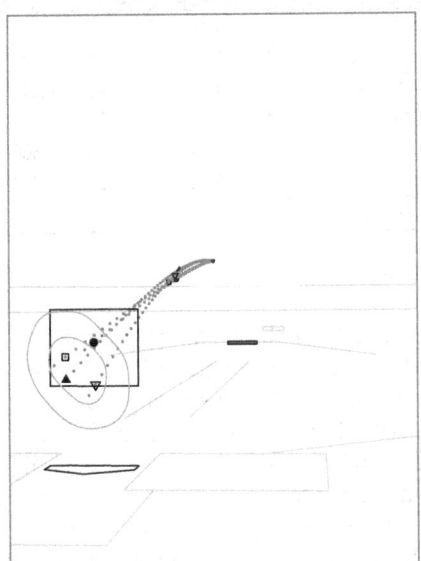	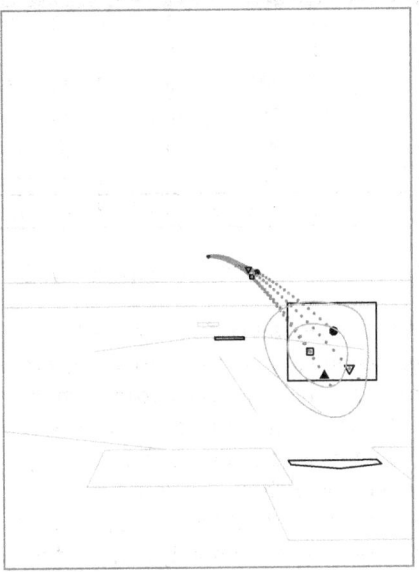

Type	Frequency	Velocity	H Movement	V Movement
● Fastball	14.3%	91.9 [98]	-8.3 [94]	-15.6 [101]
□ Sinker	33.5%	91.5 [94]	-13 [98]	-19.5 [103]
+ Cutter				
▲ Changeup	36.9%	73 [56]	-2.8 [139]	-33.9 [81]
× Splitter				
▽ Slider	15.3%	82.1 [90]	5 [100]	-35.1 [94]
◇ Curveball				
⊕ Slow Curveball				
✳ Knuckleball				
▼ Screwball				

Freddy Peralta   RHP

Born: 06/04/96   Age: 24   Bats: R   Throws: R
Height: 5'11"   Weight: 175   Origin: International Free Agent, 2013

YEAR	TEAM	LVL	AGE	W	L	SV	G	GS	IP	H	HR	BB/9	K/9	K	GB%	BABIP
2017	CAR	A+	21	1	3	0	12	8	56¹	39	6	5.0	12.5	78	39%	.268
2017	BLX	AA	21	2	5	1	13	11	63²	38	2	4.4	12.9	91	44%	.267
2018	CSP	AAA	22	6	2	0	13	13	61	49	1	4.1	12.8	87	48%	.343
2018	MIL	MLB	22	6	4	0	16	14	78¹	49	8	4.6	11.0	96	33%	.237
2019	SAN	AAA	23	0	0	0	4	0	7	4	0	3.9	21.9	17	25%	.500
2019	MIL	MLB	23	7	3	1	39	8	85	87	15	3.9	12.2	115	34%	.338
2020	MIL	MLB	24	6	5	2	47	13	97	83	14	4.1	11.2	121	36%	.296

Comparables: Jake Faria, Touki Toussaint, Enyel De Los Santos

Watching Peralta dominate the Reds in Cincinnati for eight innings on April 3rd, his second start of the campaign, it looked like he was the future of the Brewers rotation. He blew his electric fastball by Red after Red and even caught Joey Votto staring at a curveball for strike three. His 10th and final strikeout of the day came on a vicious biting curve spiked dead into the dirt to retire Yasiel Puig to end the eighth representing the go-ahead run at the plate. It's the stuff fans dream about. But Peralta lasted over five innings just once in six more starts before he was ultimately demoted to the bullpen in mid-June, where he was still mediocre at best. The curveball, so stunning that April afternoon, proved inconsistent; he couldn't locate it for a strike, and his poor control gave hitters no incentive to wave at the one in the dirt. A one-trick pony is fun to watch, but only for a little while.

YEAR	TEAM	LVL	AGE	WHIP	ERA	DRA	WARP	MPH	FB%	WHF	CSP
2017	CAR	A+	21	1.24	3.04	2.81	1.6				
2017	BLX	AA	21	1.08	2.26	2.78	1.8				
2018	CSP	AAA	22	1.26	3.10	2.80	1.9				
2018	MIL	MLB	22	1.14	4.25	5.21	0.1	94.3	77.6	12	49.2
2019	SAN	AAA	23	1.00	1.29	0.56	0.4				
2019	MIL	MLB	23	1.46	5.29	4.93	0.6	97.3	78.4	14.5	49.8
2020	MIL	MLB	24	1.31	4.09	4.12	1.7	95.8	80.4	13.9	51

Freddy Peralta, continued

Pitch Shape vs LHH

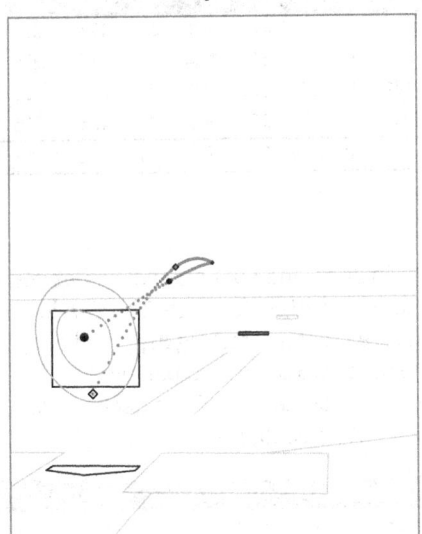

Pitch Shape vs RHH

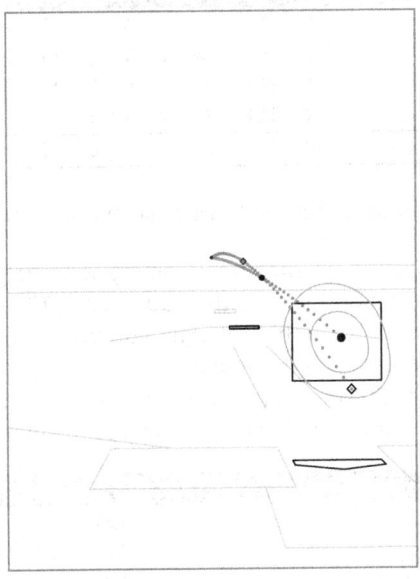

Type	Frequency	Velocity	H Movement	V Movement
● Fastball	78.4%	94.1 [105]	-6.1 [103]	-13.1 [108]
☐ Sinker				
+ Cutter				
▲ Changeup				
✕ Splitter				
▽ Slider				
◇ Curveball	20.5%	77.6 [97]	8.1 [102]	-49.8 [95]
⊕ Slow Curveball				
✱ Knuckleball				
▼ Screwball				

David Phelps RHP

Born: 10/09/86 Age: 33 Bats: R Throws: R
Height: 6'3" Weight: 200 Origin: Round 14, 2008 Draft (#440 overall)

YEAR	TEAM	LVL	AGE	W	L	SV	G	GS	IP	H	HR	BB/9	K/9	K	GB%	BABIP
2017	MIA	MLB	30	2	4	0	44	0	47	42	5	4.0	9.8	51	49%	.308
2017	SEA	MLB	30	2	1	0	10	0	8²	9	0	5.2	11.4	11	42%	.375
2019	TOR	MLB	32	0	0	0	17	1	17¹	14	3	3.6	9.3	18	31%	.262
2019	CHN	MLB	32	2	1	1	24	0	17	17	2	5.3	9.5	18	46%	.326
2020	CHN	MLB	33	2	2	0	33	0	35	35	5	3.9	8.1	31	41%	.297

Comparables: Ramon E Ramirez, Adam Warren, Bobby Parnell

Phelps returned from Tommy John surgery in June and split his season between the Blue Jays and the Cubs, facing 70-something batters for each. The ERA looks better than the rest of his components, but the most interesting aspect of his season was the shift in approach. Phelps leaned into being a flyball pitcher, tossing more cutters and curves at the cost of his sinker. The Cubs declined his option, sending him to the free-agent market at a peculiar time.

YEAR	TEAM	LVL	AGE	WHIP	ERA	DRA	WARP	MPH	FB%	WHF	CSP
2017	MIA	MLB	30	1.34	3.45	3.36	1.0	96.1	47.3	10.1	50.4
2017	SEA	MLB	30	1.62	3.12	3.99	0.1	96.2	47.3	11.5	46.2
2019	TOR	MLB	32	1.21	3.63	5.90	-0.1	93.3	39.7	6.1	43
2019	CHN	MLB	32	1.59	3.18	4.87	0.1	94.7	39.7	10.5	44.4
2020	CHN	MLB	33	1.43	4.62	4.65	0.3	94.0	42.8	9.2	45.4

David Phelps, continued

Pitch Shape vs LHH

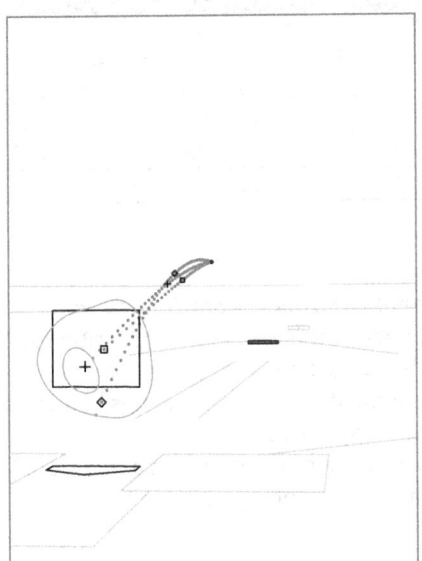

Pitch Shape vs RHH

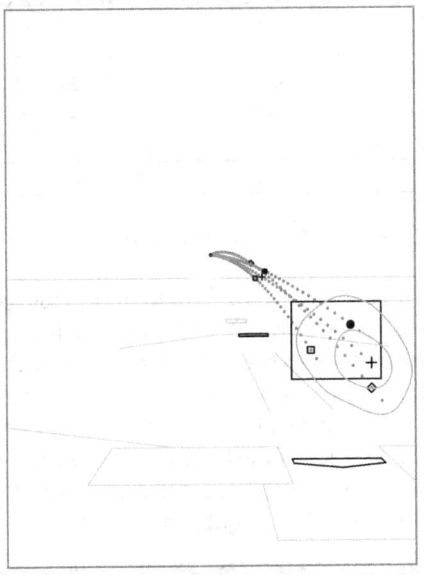

Type	Frequency	Velocity	H Movement	V Movement
● Fastball	25.9%	92.9 [101]	-4.9 [109]	-14.6 [104]
☐ Sinker	16.9%	92.7 [101]	-12.9 [99]	-18.4 [107]
+ Cutter	28.8%	89.7 [106]	2.9 [106]	-20.5 [113]
▲ Changeup				
✕ Splitter				
▽ Slider				
◇ Curveball	27.8%	80.2 [105]	8.8 [105]	-47.1 [101]
⊕ Slow Curveball				
✱ Knuckleball				
▼ Screwball				

Milwaukee Brewers 2020

Brent Suter LHP

Born: 08/29/89   Age: 30   Bats: L   Throws: L
Height: 6'5"   Weight: 195   Origin: Round 31, 2012 Draft (#965 overall)

YEAR	TEAM	LVL	AGE	W	L	SV	G	GS	IP	H	HR	BB/9	K/9	K	GB%	BABIP
2017	CSP	AAA	27	3	1	0	10	8	36^2	42	5	2.0	9.3	38	46%	.359
2017	MIL	MLB	27	3	2	0	22	14	81^2	83	8	2.4	7.1	64	46%	.306
2018	MIL	MLB	28	8	7	0	20	18	101^1	102	18	1.7	7.5	84	36%	.281
2019	SAN	AAA	29	0	0	0	4	2	11^2	4	0	1.5	13.9	18	46%	.182
2019	MIL	MLB	29	4	0	0	9	0	18^1	10	1	0.5	7.4	15	53%	.188
2020	MIL	MLB	30	4	4	0	60	3	74	70	13	2.0	7.7	63	42%	.270

Comparables: Tyler Lyons, Scott Alexander, Sam Gaviglio

Suter's 2019 was assumed to be a lost year after he underwent Tommy John surgery in July 2018. Yet he made his way back to the majors for September, and turned out to be a vital performer for the Brewers down the stretch. The question moving forward is how Milwaukee will deploy him. Suter has had some success in a starting role, but he looked perfectly suited to pitch multiple innings out of the bullpen, too. With Josh Hader settling more into a traditional role, the Brewers could use another versatile, multi-inning threat in their bullpen. Suter might just be that guy.

YEAR	TEAM	LVL	AGE	WHIP	ERA	DRA	WARP	MPH	FB%	WHF	CSP
2017	CSP	AAA	27	1.36	4.42	3.79	0.8				
2017	MIL	MLB	27	1.29	3.42	4.72	0.7	88.5	70.6	10.3	49
2018	MIL	MLB	28	1.19	4.44	5.01	0.3	89.0	68.9	11.1	50.1
2019	SAN	AAA	29	0.51	0.00	0.37	0.7				
2019	MIL	MLB	29	0.60	0.49	4.11	0.2	89.4	78.1	14.6	52.5
2020	MIL	MLB	30	1.17	3.86	4.05	1.2	88.2	70.2	11.1	50.7

Brent Suter, continued

Pitch Shape vs LHH

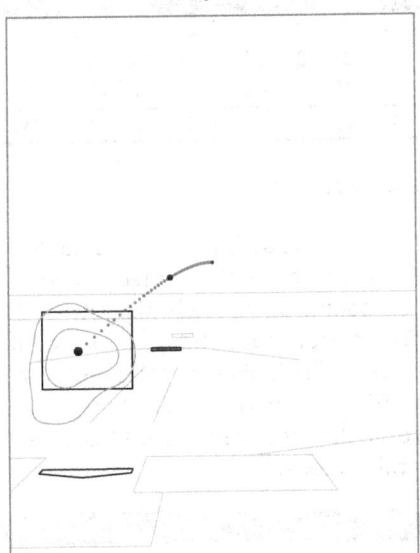

Pitch Shape vs RHH

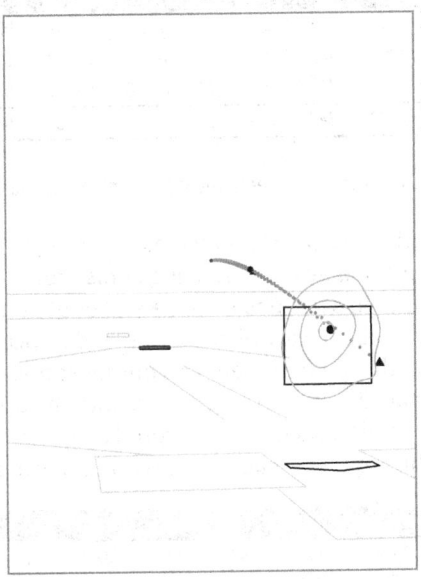

Type	Frequency	Velocity	H Movement	V Movement
● Fastball	74.2%	87.7 [87]	-1.6 [138]	-20.8 [87]
☐ Sinker	3.9%	87.8 [75]	10 [117]	-21.2 [97]
+ Cutter				
▲ Changeup	18.5%	80.7 [83]	9.2 [109]	-26.8 [102]
✕ Splitter				
▽ Slider	3.4%	74 [56]	-10.1 [121]	-49.9 [51]
◇ Curveball				
⊕ Slow Curveball				
✱ Knuckleball				
▼ Screwball				

Devin Williams RHP

Born: 09/21/94   Age: 25   Bats: R   Throws: R
Height: 6'3"   Weight: 165   Origin: Round 2, 2013 Draft (#54 overall)

YEAR	TEAM	LVL	AGE	W	L	SV	G	GS	IP	H	HR	BB/9	K/9	K	GB%	BABIP
2018	CAR	A+	23	0	3	0	14	14	34	40	2	5.8	9.3	35	38%	.380
2019	BLX	AA	24	7	2	4	31	0	53^1	34	3	4.9	12.8	76	48%	.279
2019	MIL	MLB	24	0	0	0	13	0	13^2	18	2	4.0	9.2	14	42%	.372
2020	MIL	MLB	25	2	2	0	39	0	42	41	8	3.9	8.6	40	44%	.292

Comparables: Elieser Hernandez, Domingo Germán, Jake Newberry

Williams had stagnated as a starter, but a move to the bullpen seems to have instilled new life. Looking at his profile, it's a move that makes perfect sense. Williams has posted huge strikeout numbers behind a two-pitch mix, yet struggled with wildness and endurance. The control issues, though present out of the bullpen, were less burdensome. Meanwhile, he's able to consistently air out a fastball that can touch into the upper-90s. Williams isn't going to be what the Brewers hoped he would turn into on draft day, but he might just become a high-quality reliever—and that's a win, all things considered.

YEAR	TEAM	LVL	AGE	WHIP	ERA	DRA	WARP	MPH	FB%	WHF	CSP
2018	CAR	A+	23	1.82	5.82	6.33	-0.4				
2019	BLX	AA	24	1.18	2.36	3.88	0.5				
2019	MIL	MLB	24	1.76	3.95	5.15	0.0	98.3	61	12.2	45.7
2020	MIL	MLB	25	1.42	4.98	4.93	0.2	98.0	62.5	12.5	46.8

Devin Williams, continued

Pitch Shape vs LHH

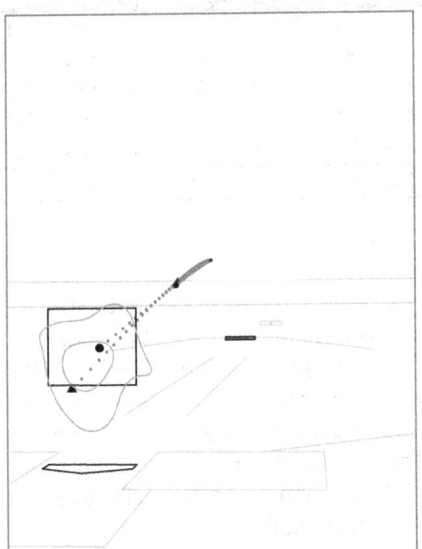

Pitch Shape vs RHH

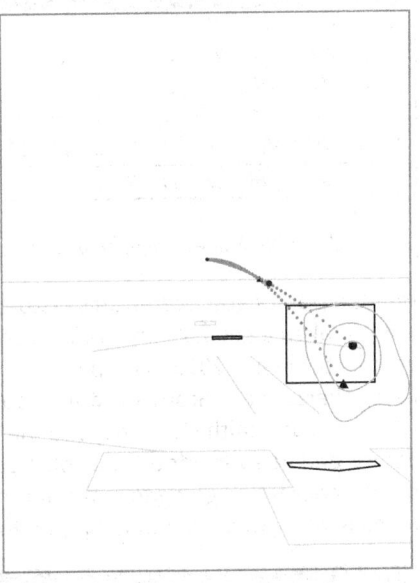

Type	Frequency	Velocity	H Movement	V Movement
● Fastball	61.0%	96.5 [112]	-11.2 [81]	-12.6 [109]
☐ Sinker				
+ Cutter				
▲ Changeup	36.6%	86.1 [103]	-16 [77]	-29.3 [95]
✕ Splitter				
▽ Slider				
◇ Curveball				
⊕ Slow Curveball				
✱ Knuckleball				
▼ Screwball				

Brandon Woodruff RHP

Born: 02/10/93 Age: 27 Bats: L Throws: R
Height: 6'4" Weight: 215 Origin: Round 11, 2014 Draft (#326 overall)

YEAR	TEAM	LVL	AGE	W	L	SV	G	GS	IP	H	HR	BB/9	K/9	K	GB%	BABIP
2017	CSP	AAA	24	6	5	0	16	16	75^1	78	8	3.0	8.4	70	49%	.323
2017	MIL	MLB	24	2	3	0	8	8	43	43	5	2.9	6.7	32	50%	.292
2018	CSP	AAA	25	3	2	0	17	17	71^1	67	8	4.0	8.6	68	50%	.296
2018	MIL	MLB	25	3	0	1	19	4	42^1	36	4	3.0	10.0	47	54%	.294
2019	MIL	MLB	26	11	3	0	22	22	121^2	109	12	2.2	10.6	143	46%	.320
2020	MIL	MLB	27	11	9	0	29	29	166	148	21	3.0	10.3	190	48%	.301

Comparables: Asher Wojciechowski, Trevor Oaks, Justin Grimm

Here's a stat for you. Woodruff's fastball coerced a whiff on 26 percent of the swings taken against it—that ranked 14th among all pitchers with 500-plus heaters thrown in 2019, right behind Max Scherzer and Jacob deGrom. Woodruff isn't Scherzer or deGrom, of course, but he looked like Milwaukee's best starter when he was healthy. The move to the rotation didn't dampen his strikeout ability, and he even added control. Woodruff will need to continue to refine his secondaries if he's going to make another All-Star Game, yet the real key to his game is going to be maintaining that top-notch fastball.

YEAR	TEAM	LVL	AGE	WHIP	ERA	DRA	WARP	MPH	FB%	WHF	CSP
2017	CSP	AAA	24	1.37	4.30	3.74	1.6				
2017	MIL	MLB	24	1.33	4.81	5.65	0.0	96.7	60.5	9.8	46.2
2018	CSP	AAA	25	1.39	4.04	3.59	1.6				
2018	MIL	MLB	25	1.18	3.61	3.16	0.9	97.9	64.1	11.3	50.1
2019	MIL	MLB	26	1.14	3.62	3.23	3.4	98.4	64.1	13.1	49.3
2020	MIL	MLB	27	1.22	3.57	3.69	3.9	97.6	64.3	12.4	49.4

Brandon Woodruff, continued

Pitch Shape vs LHH

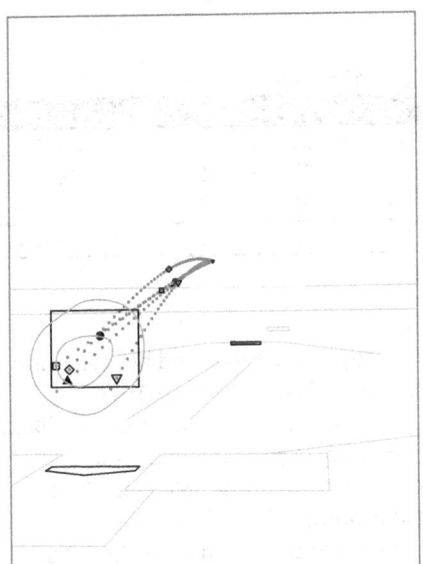

Pitch Shape vs RHH

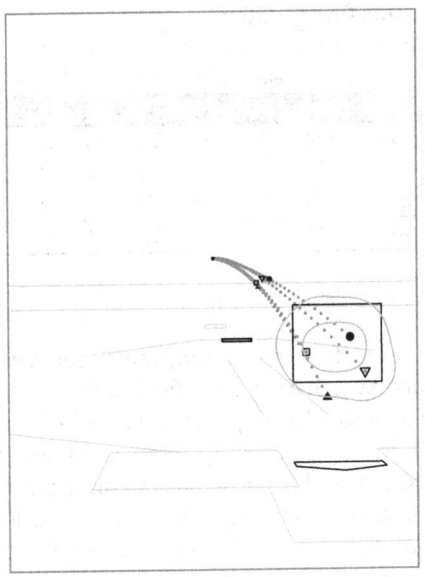

Type	Frequency	Velocity	H Movement	V Movement
● Fastball	40.8%	96.8 [113]	-7.5 [97]	-12.7 [108]
☐ Sinker	23.3%	96.3 [119]	-13.3 [96]	-16.4 [114]
+ Cutter				
▲ Changeup	14.2%	87.4 [108]	-13.8 [88]	-24.8 [108]
✕ Splitter				
▽ Slider	19.5%	88.9 [119]	3.4 [93]	-28.5 [113]
◇ Curveball				
⊕ Slow Curveball				
✻ Knuckleball				
▼ Screwball				

PLAYER COMMENTS WITHOUT GRAPHS

Lucas Erceg 3B
Born: 05/01/95   Age: 25   Bats: L   Throws: R
Height: 6'3"   Weight: 210   Origin: Round 2, 2016 Draft (#46 overall)

YEAR	TEAM	LVL	AGE	PA	R	2B	3B	HR	RBI	BB	K	SB	CS	AVG/OBP/SLG
2017	CAR	A+	22	538	66	33	1	15	81	35	95	2	3	.256/.307/.417
2018	BLX	AA	23	508	52	21	1	13	51	37	82	3	1	.248/.306/.382
2019	SAN	AAA	24	406	55	17	1	15	52	44	102	2	2	.218/.305/.398
2020	MIL	MLB	25	251	26	12	1	9	30	19	69	0	0	.224/.285/.394

Comparables: Kelvin Gutierrez, Jordy Mercer, Jefry Marte

Even before the season, some scouts were ready to see Erceg and his near-elite arm switch from the infield to the mound. After a disappointing 2019 that suggested he might have peaked as a hitter, more and more evaluators are likely to join the chorus. Erceg doesn't have the mobility to play anywhere but a corner, and while he has the raw power to make it work, his plate discipline hampers his overall offensive upside. Perhaps another year of working with Driveline Baseball can help Erceg, but there's a real chance that this time next year he'll be working with them on his fastball-curveball combination.

YEAR	TEAM	LVL	AGE	PA	DRC+	VORP	BABIP	BRR	FRAA	WARP
2017	CAR	A+	22	538	100	11.3	.287	-1.6	3B(97): -0.6	1.3
2018	BLX	AA	23	508	96	8.5	.274	-0.4	3B(117): -0.7	1.5
2019	SAN	AAA	24	406	65	-1.6	.259	-2.0	3B(84): 7.9, 1B(18): 1.8	0.4
2020	MIL	MLB	25	251	77	0.2	.279	-0.4	3B 1, 1B 0	0.2

Mario Feliciano C

Born: 11/20/98 Age: 21 Bats: R Throws: R
Height: 6'1" Weight: 195 Origin: Round 2, 2016 Draft (#75 overall)

YEAR	TEAM	LVL	AGE	PA	R	2B	3B	HR	RBI	BB	K	SB	CS	AVG/OBP/SLG
2017	WIS	A	18	446	47	16	2	4	36	34	72	10	2	.251/.320/.331
2018	CAR	A+	19	165	20	7	1	3	12	13	59	2	0	.205/.282/.329
2019	CAR	A+	20	482	62	25	4	19	81	29	139	2	1	.273/.324/.477
2020	MIL	MLB	21	251	23	11	1	7	27	15	78	1	0	.223/.277/.368

Comparables: Cole Tucker, Gary Sánchez, Engel Beltre

Despite Feliciano being just 20 years old, 2019 was a critical season for him. The previous campaign had been a bust, as he had dealt with numerous injuries and had struggled in his sporadic appearances to adapt to High-A pitching. A second rough campaign in a row would have threatened his prospect status. Feliciano instead bounced back and reminded everyone why he merited a second-round selection in the first place, earning Carolina League MVP honors thanks to his budding home-run swing. Providing he can continue to hone his defensive skills—including an above-average arm—he has the potential to give the Brewers everything they want and need, baby: good glove and offensive projection. Make Feliciano your selection for Milwaukee's catcher of the future.

YEAR	TEAM	LVL	AGE	PA	DRC+	VORP	BABIP	BRR	FRAA	WARP
2017	WIS	A	18	446	88	11.2	.297	1.4	C(78): -2.8	0.9
2018	CAR	A+	19	165	51	0.4	.318	0.5	C(25): -0.6	-0.2
2019	CAR	A+	20	482	119	19.0	.351	-5.1	C(60): -0.4	1.7
2020	MIL	MLB	21	251	70	-1.8	.304	-0.3	C -1	-0.3

Milwaukee Brewers 2020

Jacob Nottingham C
Born: 04/03/95 Age: 25 Bats: R Throws: R
Height: 6'2" Weight: 230 Origin: Round 6, 2013 Draft (#167 overall)

YEAR	TEAM	LVL	AGE	PA	R	2B	3B	HR	RBI	BB	K	SB	CS	AVG/OBP/SLG
2017	BLX	AA	22	385	37	21	2	9	48	37	87	7	3	.209/.326/.369
2018	CSP	AAA	23	196	33	10	2	10	36	14	59	2	1	.281/.347/.528
2018	MIL	MLB	23	24	2	1	0	0	0	4	8	0	0	.200/.333/.250
2019	SAN	AAA	24	332	40	21	0	5	40	28	95	6	1	.231/.313/.355
2019	MIL	MLB	24	7	1	0	0	1	4	0	2	0	0	.333/.429/.833
2020	MIL	MLB	25	42	4	2	0	1	5	3	14	0	0	.217/.288/.379

Comparables: Gary Sánchez, Brett Phillips, Kyle Skipworth

Milwaukee's surprise Yasmani Grandal signing sealed Nottingham's assignment to Triple-A before he had a chance to win a big-league job. Grandal's one-year deal set the table for Nottingham to go back to the minors, dominate and position himself for a position in the 2020 startling lineup. Yet at a time when every other Triple-A hitter produced more power, Nottingham went counterculture. We're generally fans of subversion, but it's not a great idea when you're a bat-only catcher whose entire stock hinges on the one thing you're no longer doing. He'll try again in 2020, right along with the rest of us.

YEAR	TEAM	P. COUNT	FRM RUNS	BLK RUNS	THRW RUNS	TOT RUNS
2017	BLX	11440	7.2	-1.7	0.0	5.8
2018	CSP	4056	1.5	-1.1	-0.2	0.0
2018	MIL	937	-0.7	0.2	0.0	-0.5
2019	MIL	163	0.0	-0.1	0.0	0.4
2019	SAN	8544	12.0	0.0	-0.9	11.4
2020	MIL	1298	-0.7	0.0	-0.1	-0.8

YEAR	TEAM	LVL	AGE	PA	DRC+	VORP	BABIP	BRR	FRAA	WARP
2017	BLX	AA	22	385	104	11.9	.255	-3.0	C(83): 4.7, 1B(13): -0.8	2.0
2018	CSP	AAA	23	196	96	10.7	.367	-0.6	C(32): -0.3, 1B(9): 0.0	0.6
2018	MIL	MLB	23	24	71	0.7	.333	-0.1	C(8): -0.5	0.0
2019	SAN	AAA	24	332	74	3.3	.318	-1.4	C(65): 11.7, 1B(8): 0.2	1.4
2019	MIL	MLB	24	7	97	0.3	.333	0.0	C(6): -0.3, 1B(1): 0.0	0.0
2020	MIL	MLB	25	42	76	0.6	.297	-0.1	C -1	0.0

Corey Ray OF

Born: 09/22/94 Age: 25 Bats: L Throws: L
Height: 6'0" Weight: 195 Origin: Round 1, 2016 Draft (#5 overall)

YEAR	TEAM	LVL	AGE	PA	R	2B	3B	HR	RBI	BB	K	SB	CS	AVG/OBP/SLG
2017	CAR	A+	22	503	56	29	4	7	48	48	156	24	10	.238/.311/.367
2018	BLX	AA	23	600	86	32	7	27	74	60	176	37	7	.239/.323/.477
2019	BLX	AA	24	46	5	3	0	0	0	6	14	3	2	.250/.348/.325
2019	SAN	AAA	24	230	23	8	0	7	21	20	89	3	1	.188/.261/.329
2020	MIL	MLB	25	251	23	13	1	6	24	19	98	8	3	.197/.262/.336

Comparables: Joe Benson, Michael A. Taylor, Anthony Alford

That whole "striking out 30 percent of the time" thing came back to bite Ray in a big way in 2019, as did Milwaukee's change of Triple-A venue, from Colorado Springs to San Antonio. The result was by far his worst season in the minors, including the ignominious accomplishment of accumulating more strikeouts than total bases. The power Ray showed in 2018 is impossible to ignore, and he will be just 25 in 2020. A time of reckoning (Ray-gnarök?) will come shortly if he can't patch the holes in his swing.

YEAR	TEAM	LVL	AGE	PA	DRC+	VORP	BABIP	BRR	FRAA	WARP
2017	CAR	A+	22	503	96	7.1	.346	-2.5	CF(80): 5.5, RF(24): 0.9	1.6
2018	BLX	AA	23	600	119	35.8	.303	0.5	CF(126): 1.8, LF(6): 1.4	3.6
2019	BLX	AA	24	46	116	1.0	.385	0.1	CF(10): 1.6, LF(1): -0.2	0.4
2019	SAN	AAA	24	230	45	-1.2	.283	-0.4	CF(40): -5.0, RF(8): -1.3	-1.2
2020	MIL	MLB	25	251	58	-5.0	.313	0.5	CF 2, RF 0	-0.3

Tyrone Taylor OF

Born: 01/22/94   Age: 26   Bats: R   Throws: R
Height: 6'0"   Weight: 185   Origin: Round 2, 2012 Draft (#92 overall)

YEAR	TEAM	LVL	AGE	PA	R	2B	3B	HR	RBI	BB	K	SB	CS	AVG/OBP/SLG
2017	BRR	RK	23	26	6	1	0	4	7	3	3	2	0	.435/.500/1.000
2017	BLX	AA	23	95	15	6	1	1	6	8	18	2	1	.247/.316/.376
2018	CSP	AAA	24	481	73	23	9	20	80	27	74	13	4	.278/.321/.504
2019	SAN	AAA	25	375	44	20	1	14	59	28	85	5	0	.269/.334/.461
2019	MIL	MLB	25	12	1	2	0	0	1	1	1	0	0	.400/.500/.600
2020	MIL	MLB	26	119	13	5	0	4	14	7	27	2	1	.231/.287/.401

Comparables: Rey Fuentes, Gorkys Hernández, Tzu-Wei Lin

Taylor's numbers look more or less the same from 2018 to 2019, but the context is key: Colorado Springs, the Brewers' 2018 Triple-A home, is arguably the most hitter-friendly park in professional baseball (or, at least, this side of High Desert). Taylor showed improved discipline and hardly suffered at all from a power perspective after the move to San Antonio. Consider those both good signs for his future. It can be easy with a player like Taylor to lament the fact that he hasn't reached the lofty heights his tools suggested he could, but he might be just what Milwaukee needs in 2020: a strong defensive outfielder capable of covering all three outfield spots.

YEAR	TEAM	LVL	AGE	PA	DRC+	VORP	BABIP	BRR	FRAA	WARP
2017	BRR	RK	23	26	215	7.3	.375	0.3	CF(7): -0.8	0.3
2017	BLX	AA	23	95	85	1.8	.299	1.1	LF(8): 0.7, RF(7): 2.5	0.5
2018	CSP	AAA	24	481	99	17.6	.292	2.3	CF(56): 0.5, LF(39): 7.2	2.5
2019	SAN	AAA	25	375	92	12.0	.317	0.3	RF(46): 1.6, CF(43): 8.5	1.7
2019	MIL	MLB	25	12	89	0.3	.444	-0.4	RF(8): -0.1, CF(3): -0.3	0.0
2020	MIL	MLB	26	119	81	0.8	.268	-0.1	CF 1, RF 0	0.2

Brice Turang MI

Born: 11/21/99 Age: 20 Bats: L Throws: R
Height: 6'0" Weight: 173 Origin: Round 1, 2018 Draft (#21 overall)

YEAR	TEAM	LVL	AGE	PA	R	2B	3B	HR	RBI	BB	K	SB	CS	AVG/OBP/SLG
2018	BRR	RK	18	57	11	2	0	0	7	9	6	8	1	.319/.421/.362
2018	HEL	RK	18	135	26	4	1	1	11	22	28	6	1	.268/.385/.348
2019	WIS	A	19	357	57	13	4	2	31	49	54	21	4	.287/.384/.376
2019	CAR	A+	19	207	25	6	2	1	6	34	47	9	1	.200/.338/.276
2020	MIL	MLB	20	251	23	10	1	4	23	25	60	5	1	.230/.310/.338

Comparables: J.P. Crawford, Gavin Lux, Ehire Adrianza

Milwaukee's top prospect, Turang didn't respond well to a promotion to High-A. That's understandable, given he was three-plus years younger than the average competition he faced. His lack of pop and devotion to walking leaves us thinking about Cliff Pennington. That's supposed to be a compliment—Pennington had a long, and at times fruitful career—but we understand if you instead take it as an indictment of the Brewers' farm system.

YEAR	TEAM	LVL	AGE	PA	DRC+	VORP	BABIP	BRR	FRAA	WARP
2018	BRR	RK	18	57	153	4.5	.357	0.0	SS(12): 2.0	0.7
2018	HEL	RK	18	135	119	9.8	.345	1.7	SS(23): -0.1, 2B(5): -0.1	0.6
2019	WIS	A	19	357	142	25.1	.339	3.2	SS(43): 0.6, 2B(28): 0.9	3.2
2019	CAR	A+	19	207	99	2.4	.268	1.6	SS(35): -2.6, 2B(5): -0.8	0.6
2020	MIL	MLB	20	251	76	0.8	.297	0.4	SS -1, 2B -1	-0.1

Aaron Ashby LHP

Born: 05/24/98 Age: 22 Bats: R Throws: L
Height: 6'2" Weight: 181 Origin: Round 4, 2018 Draft (#125 overall)

YEAR	TEAM	LVL	AGE	W	L	SV	G	GS	IP	H	HR	BB/9	K/9	K	GB%	BABIP
2018	HEL	RK	20	1	2	1	6	3	20^1	18	3	3.5	8.4	19	52%	.273
2018	WIS	A	20	1	1	0	7	7	37^1	40	1	2.2	11.3	47	52%	.398
2019	WIS	A	21	3	4	0	11	10	61	47	4	4.1	11.8	80	49%	.319
2019	CAR	A+	21	2	6	0	13	13	65	54	1	4.4	7.6	55	50%	.283
2020	MIL	MLB	22	2	2	0	33	0	35	34	5	4.1	8.1	32	46%	.293

Comparables: Justin Wilson, Blake Snell, Yenssy Diaz

The nephew of Andy, who played 14 years for various National League squads, Aaron showed he wasn't just a nepotism pick in his first full season in professional baseball. Rather, he earned the organization's award for the top minor-league pitcher for his success across both A-ball levels. This Ashby can only hope that his control improves with age, the way his uncle's did. Should that happen, he might stick in the rotation. Otherwise, he's looking at life in the pen—but what a life it could be.

YEAR	TEAM	LVL	AGE	WHIP	ERA	DRA	WARP	MPH	FB%	WHF	CSP
2018	HEL	RK	20	1.28	6.20	2.95	0.7				
2018	WIS	A	20	1.31	2.17	4.19	0.5				
2019	WIS	A	21	1.23	3.54	4.45	0.5				
2019	CAR	A+	21	1.32	3.46	4.81	0.2				
2020	MIL	MLB	22	1.43	4.79	4.81	0.2				

Corey Knebel RHP

Born: 11/26/91   Age: 28   Bats: R   Throws: R
Height: 6'4"   Weight: 220   Origin: Round 1, 2013 Draft (#39 overall)

YEAR	TEAM	LVL	AGE	W	L	SV	G	GS	IP	H	HR	BB/9	K/9	K	GB%	BABIP
2017	MIL	MLB	25	1	4	39	76	0	76	48	6	4.7	14.9	126	39%	.311
2018	MIL	MLB	26	4	3	16	57	0	55¹	38	7	3.6	14.3	88	50%	.304
2020	MIL	MLB	28	2	2	2	34	0	36	31	6	4.1	12.4	49	44%	.308

Comparables: Carl Edwards Jr., Keone Kela, Bruce Rondón

Is a tired arm ever really just a tired arm? That was the diagnosis for Knebel on March 20th, just a few days after he pushed through his longest outing of spring training—a five-out appearance, the likes of which the Brewers were hoping to rely on long into the dog days of summer. "Just giving it a break," Knebel told reporters. He wouldn't throw a single major league inning in 2019, as that "tired arm" evolved in to a UCL issue, and he underwent Tommy John surgery later in the month. Perhaps we shouldn't be too surprised; Knebel's delivery is violent, and he threw more innings in 2017 and 2018 combined than any two-year stretch in his career, all while pumping his average fastball velocity up from 95 to over 97. Knebel's recovery was on track as of the end of the season, so he should be back sometime in 2020.

YEAR	TEAM	LVL	AGE	WHIP	ERA	DRA	WARP	MPH	FB%	WHF	CSP
2017	MIL	MLB	25	1.16	1.78	3.09	1.8	99.2	71.8	15.4	47.4
2018	MIL	MLB	26	1.08	3.58	2.53	1.5	98.8	70.9	14.5	49.2
2020	MIL	MLB	28	1.31	4.20	4.22	0.5	98.4	71.8	15	48.7

Josh Lindblom RHP

Born: 06/15/87   Age: 33   Bats: R   Throws: R
Height: 6'4"   Weight: 240   Origin: Round 2, 2008 Draft (#61 overall)

YEAR	TEAM	LVL	AGE	W	L	SV	G	GS	IP	H	HR	BB/9	K/9	K	GB%	BABIP
2017	IND	AAA	30	0	2	0	17	4	37^2	37	5	1.9	7.9	33	34%	.294
2017	PIT	MLB	30	0	0	0	4	0	10^1	18	0	2.6	8.7	10	42%	.474
2020	MIL	MLB	33	8	9	0	26	26	135	145	28	2.8	6.7	100	36%	.288

Comparables: Jeff Manship, Chaz Roe, Logan Kensing

Denis Johnson once suggested that the key to making a tree treat you as a friend was to leave it alone. "After the blade bit in," Johnson wrote, "you had yourself a war." The Brewers have, for years, gotten away with a so-so-looking rotation by leaving it alone, save for a late-season addition here and there. That changed over the winter winter. They shipped out Zach Davies and Chase Anderson and non-tendered Jimmy Nelson—all for financial reasons—only to eschew big-named replacements and instead add Eric Lauer, Brett Anderson and Lindblom, who performed nicely in his three seasons spent in Korea. He doesn't throw hard and he'll be doing well if he's a league-average starter, but the Brewers are used to courting war with their budget-saving maneuvers. Now that the blade has bit in, the Brewers are just hoping for a WARP.

YEAR	TEAM	LVL	AGE	WHIP	ERA	DRA	WARP	MPH	FB%	WHF	CSP
2017	IND	AAA	30	1.19	4.06	4.32	0.5				
2017	PIT	MLB	30	2.03	7.84	6.99	-0.2	92.4	53.8	11.3	46.1
2020	MIL	MLB	33	1.39	5.31	5.35	0.7	91.4	53.1	11.2	45.6

Trey Supak RHP

Born: 05/31/96 Age: 24 Bats: R Throws: R
Height: 6'5" Weight: 240 Origin: Round 2, 2014 Draft (#73 overall)

YEAR	TEAM	LVL	AGE	W	L	SV	G	GS	IP	H	HR	BB/9	K/9	K	GB%	BABIP
2017	WIS	A	21	2	2	0	8	7	41	21	1	2.2	11.6	53	36%	.235
2017	CAR	A+	21	3	4	1	15	11	72^1	65	12	3.5	7.1	57	34%	.261
2018	CAR	A+	22	2	1	0	9	9	51	37	2	2.8	8.5	48	38%	.269
2018	BLX	AA	22	6	6	0	16	16	86^2	74	4	2.9	7.8	75	45%	.286
2019	BLX	AA	23	11	4	0	20	20	122^2	84	6	1.7	6.7	91	47%	.226
2019	SAN	AAA	23	1	2	0	7	7	30	41	6	2.7	8.1	27	37%	.387
2020	MIL	MLB	24	3	3	0	10	10	46	46	8	3.8	6.4	33	42%	.274

Comparables: Jorge López, Ronald Bolaños, Chase De Jong

A rough introduction to the Pacific Coast League put to rest talk of Supak arriving in Milwaukee in 2019. How rough was it? Supak allowed just as many home runs in his 20 starts in Double-A as he did in seven starts in Triple-A. Woof. The altered baseball undoubtedly is a partial culprit, but Supak has long been considered a potential bullpen candidate due to merely average stuff. The Brewers originally acquired him (*and* Keon Broxton) for Jason Rogers, so whatever happens won't result in trader's remorse.

YEAR	TEAM	LVL	AGE	WHIP	ERA	DRA	WARP	MPH	FB%	WHF	CSP
2017	WIS	A	21	0.76	1.76	2.08	1.5				
2017	CAR	A+	21	1.29	4.60	4.93	0.2				
2018	CAR	A+	22	1.04	1.76	3.14	1.3				
2018	BLX	AA	22	1.18	2.91	4.05	1.3				
2019	BLX	AA	23	0.87	2.20	3.19	2.6				
2019	SAN	AAA	23	1.67	9.30	8.27	-0.4				
2020	MIL	MLB	24	1.42	5.03	5.05	0.4				

Bobby Wahl   RHP

Born: 03/21/92   Age: 28   Bats: R   Throws: R
Height: 6'2"   Weight: 210   Origin: Round 5, 2013 Draft (#161 overall)

YEAR	TEAM	LVL	AGE	W	L	SV	G	GS	IP	H	HR	BB/9	K/9	K	GB%	BABIP
2017	NAS	AAA	25	1	1	3	11	0	13	13	3	3.5	15.2	22	23%	.357
2017	OAK	MLB	25	0	0	0	7	0	7^2	8	0	4.7	9.4	8	22%	.348
2018	NAS	AAA	26	3	2	11	34	1	39^2	17	2	3.9	14.7	65	42%	.224
2018	NYN	MLB	26	0	1	0	7	0	5^1	9	2	6.8	11.8	7	17%	.438
2020	MIL	MLB	28	1	1	0	23	0	24	24	5	4.2	9.3	25	36%	.293

Comparables: Jimmie Sherfy, Colton Murray, Giovanny Gallegos

Ligaments are fickle beasts. It wasn't the UCL that doomed Wahl—as you might expect from a reliever capable of chucking 98 mph fastballs and biting mid-80s curveballs—instead, it was the ACL in his right knee, his push-off leg, that gave away as he delivered a pitch in a spring training game. If that sounds like a freak injury to you...well, history agrees: According to MLB's central injury database, Wahl is just the third player to suffer such an injury to his back knee as the direct result of throwing a pitch. It's too bad for various reasons, including the possibility that Wahl would have made for a nifty addition to the Brewers bullpen; his 42.7 percent strikeout rate and 20.7 percent whiff rate in Triple-A in 2018 made him one of the more enticing young relief arms out there. Provided he makes a full recovery, he should factor into their 2020 bullpen.

YEAR	TEAM	LVL	AGE	WHIP	ERA	DRA	WARP	MPH	FB%	WHF	CSP
2017	NAS	AAA	25	1.38	4.15	2.91	0.3				
2017	OAK	MLB	25	1.57	4.70	7.51	-0.2	97.4	78.6	11	51.2
2018	NAS	AAA	26	0.86	2.27	1.91	1.5				
2018	NYN	MLB	26	2.44	10.12	4.11	0.0	98.3	72.3	14.3	51.7
2020	MIL	MLB	28	1.46	5.43	5.33	0.0	97.2	75.9	12.8	51.8

LINEOUTS

Hitters

HITTER	POS	TEAM	LVL	AGE	PA	R	2B	3B	HR	RBI	BB	K	SB	CS	AVG/OBP/SLG	DRC+	WARP
Pablo Abreu	OF	BRR	Rk	19	62	7	4	1	1	10	6	21	0	0	.226/.306/.396	50	-0.2
	OF	WIS	A	19	113	13	4	1	0	11	9	35	3	0	.186/.248/.245	54	0.3
Micah Bello	OF	CSP	Rk+	18	198	30	9	3	6	20	18	47	5	4	.232/.308/.418	73	0.2
Thomas Dillard	C	WIS	A	21	216	27	6	0	6	24	43	50	7	0	.246/.398/.386	144	1.2
Larry Ernesto	OF	BRR	Rk	18	132	15	3	0	2	9	7	59	5	1	.172/.229/.246	4	-0.6
David Freitas	C	SEA	MLB	30	4	1	0	0	0	1	1	0	0	0	.000/.250/.000	95	0.0
	C	TAC	AAA	30	25	4	2	0	0	5	5	6	0	0	.278/.480/.389	152	2.5
	C	SAN	AAA	30	359	51	21	0	12	76	42	49	0	1	.387/.459/.571	161	3.4
	C	MIL	MLB	30	16	1	0	0	0	0	3	5	0	0	.077/.250/.077	82	0.0
Ryon Healy	3B	SEA	MLB	27	187	24	16	0	7	26	13	40	0	0	.237/.289/.456	95	-0.1
Payton Henry	C	CAR	A+	22	482	49	22	1	14	75	26	142	1	1	.242/.315/.395	98	1.4
Nick Kahle	C	CSP	Rk+	21	163	25	11	1	6	25	20	36	2	1	.255/.350/.475	125	0.7
Tristen Lutz	OF	CAR	A+	20	477	62	24	3	13	54	46	137	3	2	.255/.335/.419	109	0.9
Mark Mathias	2B	COH	AAA	24	478	62	31	2	12	59	51	91	13	2	.269/.355/.442	105	1.8
Jace Peterson	2B	BAL	MLB	29	108	14	3	1	2	11	6	24	4	1	.220/.269/.330	80	0.5
	2B	NOR	AAA	29	377	58	25	5	10	46	46	56	13	3	.313/.398/.512	131	2.7
Carlos Rodriguez	OF	CSP	Rk+	18	157	20	3	1	3	12	4	20	4	6	.331/.350/.424	120	0.7

Pablo Abreu, signed out of the Dominican Republic for $800,000 in 2016, has a good frame and power potential, but desperately needs to adjust his swing for the soft stuff. ⓧ When 19th century Californians found mica below, they were bummed about fool's gold. When the present day Brewers found **Micah Bello**, they hoped to unearth an eventual everyday outfielder. ⓧ One can only hope fifth-rounder **Thomas Dillard** is half as funny as former reliever Tim Dillard. This Dillard won't have all that free time in the bullpen to construct his routine—his future lies behind the plate or in the outfield. ⓧ Five-tool potential earned **Larry Ernesto** a $1.7 million signing bonus out of the Dominican Republic. You'll have a different job by the time he reaches the majors. ⓧ **David Freitas** appeared in 16 games with the Brewers, and every single time as a pinch-hitter. He's known more for his mitt than his stick, so you do the math on how that worked out. ⓧ The poorly named **Ryon Healy** had his season disrupted by nagging back and hip injuries, which led to season-ending surgery. The power is still there, but the only way you'll see "patient" and Healy in the same sentence is when discussing his medical records. ⓧ **Payton Henry** has a Russell Branyan-sized strikeout problem to solve, but any catcher with his kind of pop is worth keeping eyes on. He could be the next Sam Huff, or he could be the next Sam Hunt if this whole 'ball thing fails. ⓧ With many catchers, the question is if their defense will hold up as they climb the ladder; for **Nick Kahle**, the defense was what attracted the Brewers. The power and discipline the fourth-rounder showed in his first full season, then, are quite encouraging. ⓧ **Tristen Lutz** produced a near duplicate of his 2018 line, which is more impressive than it sounds given his advancement up the ladder. He has the physical tools to be a starting-caliber outfielder, so now we just have to wait for his contact or power to take the next step. Or for the tides to rise. That's an option, too. ⓧ Acquired from Cleveland in November, **Mark Mathias** joins a slew of infielders for whom major-league playing time would mean disaster in Milwaukee. ⓧ There's a three percent chance **Jace Peterson**'s next club will unlock something in his swing that adds some power and makes him a massive breakout slugger, and a 97 percent chance that club will also put off selecting his contract from Triple-A because he'll cost too much. ⓧ Big ticket 2017 international signing **Carlos Rodriguez** has hit for big average in the lowest levels of the minors over the last two years. He's got limited power, but has potential to be a nifty hit/speed/defense center fielder.

Pitchers

PITCHER	TEAM	LVL	AGE	W	L	SV	G	GS	IP	H	HR	BB/9	K/9	K	GB%	WHIP	ERA	DRA	WARP
Zack Brown	SAN	AAA	24	3	7	0	25	23	116^2	138	16	4.9	7.6	98	54%	1.73	5.79	6.53	0.2
Jacob Faria	DUR	AAA	25	6	2	1	23	7	59^2	55	8	3.9	11.2	74	37%	1.36	4.07	4.10	1.3
	SAN	AAA	25	1	1	0	6	0	7^2	8	1	5.9	9.4	8	43%	1.70	2.35	6.43	0.0
	MIL	MLB	25	0	1	0	9	0	8^2	18	3	5.2	8.3	8	41%	2.65	11.42	6.62	-0.1
	TBA	MLB	25	0	0	0	7	0	10	10	2	6.3	9.9	11	45%	1.70	2.70	5.89	-0.1
J.P. Feyereisen	SWB	AAA	26	10	2	7	40	0	61^1	37	6	4.5	13.8	94	38%	1.11	2.49	2.08	2.5
Deolis Guerra	SAN	AAA	30	4	0	0	45	1	66^2	43	5	2.2	11.9	88	44%	0.88	1.89	1.15	3.3
	MIL	MLB	30	0	0	0	1	0	0^2	4	1	0.0	0.0	0	0%	6.00	54.00	5.29	0.0
Jay Jackson	SAN	AAA	31	5	2	8	34	0	40^2	28	1	2.2	12.0	54	41%	0.93	1.33	1.11	2.0
	MIL	MLB	31	1	0	0	28	0	30^1	22	6	5.3	13.9	47	38%	1.32	4.45	3.96	0.5
Jeremy Jeffress	MIL	MLB	31	3	4	1	48	0	52	54	5	2.9	8.0	46	49%	1.37	5.02	4.80	0.3
Antoine Kelly	BRB	Rk	19	0	0	0	9	9	28^2	21	0	1.6	12.9	41	47%	0.91	1.26	1.57	1.4
Shelby Miller	BRR	Rk	28	0	1	0	2	2	9	4	0	1.0	14.0	14	67%	0.56	2.00	3.45	0.3
	SAN	AAA	28	1	2	0	5	5	20^2	17	1	7.0	8.7	20	44%	1.60	4.79	4.36	0.5
	TEX	MLB	28	1	3	0	19	8	44	58	8	5.9	6.1	30	41%	1.98	8.59	9.08	-1.6
Angel Perdomo	BLX	AA	25	2	0	0	7	0	15^1	6	0	4.7	12.3	21	46%	0.91	1.17	2.59	0.4
	SAN	AAA	25	3	2	1	40	0	54	47	8	6.3	14.3	86	34%	1.57	5.17	4.14	1.1
Drew Rasmussen	CAR	A+	23	0	0	0	4	4	11^1	7	0	1.6	12.7	16	52%	0.79	1.59	2.57	0.3
	BLX	AA	23	1	3	0	22	18	61	49	4	4.3	11.4	77	48%	1.28	3.54	4.29	0.5
Ethan Small	WIS	A	22	0	2	0	5	5	18	11	0	2.0	15.5	31	32%	0.83	1.00	2.50	0.6
Braden Webb	BRR	Rk	24	0	1	0	5	5	8	1	0	5.6	14.6	13	46%	0.75	2.25	0.94	0.4
	CAR	A+	24	1	2	0	8	8	36^2	23	2	6.1	7.6	31	35%	1.31	3.44	3.69	0.6
	BLX	AA	24	1	4	0	6	5	15	15	2	9.0	7.8	13	32%	2.00	9.00	7.52	-0.5
Aaron Wilkerson	SAN	AAA	30	8	2	0	17	17	76^1	62	10	3.4	9.6	81	38%	1.19	3.42	2.44	3.2
	MIL	MLB	30	0	0	0	8	0	16	25	4	5.1	6.2	11	38%	2.12	7.31	8.11	-0.5
Taylor Williams	SAN	AAA	27	3	3	6	46	0	54	40	8	3.5	9.5	57	56%	1.13	2.83	2.59	1.9
	MIL	MLB	27	1	1	0	10	0	14^2	22	1	4.3	9.2	15	61%	1.98	9.82	4.96	0.1
Eric Yardley	ELP	AAA	28	0	2	7	43	0	63^2	60	3	2.0	7.4	52	64%	1.16	2.83	2.01	2.6
	SDN	MLB	28	0	1	0	10	0	11^2	12	1	2.3	5.4	7	66%	1.29	2.31	4.37	0.1

Between "The Owl" and the combination of the altered ball and the PCL, it just wasn't a good year for anyone named **Zack Brown**. This one will try to regain some prospect shine in 2020. ⓧ **Jake Faria**'s lack of velocity forces him to nibble a bit, but there's a fine line between nibbling and lacking control. Faria vaulted over it at both Triple-A and the majors in 2019. ⓧ Milwaukee finally freed **J.P. Feyereisen** from the overstock of interesting Yankee arms just before the Rule 5 Draft. A long history of high-minors success (and nominative determinism) suggests he could be an effective Feyer Man if give a chance. ⓧ Dominating Triple-A (as a 30-year-old, mind you) landed **Deolis Guerra** back in the majors for the first time since 2017—for two outs, anyway. Still, that's more than Johan Santana, Kevin Mulvey, Carlos Gómez and Phil Humber did in 2019. ⚾ **Jay Jackson's** fastball-slider combination was fierce against right-handed batters, but he chose to return to Japan rather than follow the Joe Smith career path. ⚾ **Jeremy Jeffress'** food truck, JJ's Bread and Butter, served meals this year at Miller Park, which is odd because opposing batters seemed to prefer eating up his pitches. ⚾ Ever moths to the flames that are young, tall pitchers, the Brewers selected 6-foot-6 **Antoine Kelly** in the second round. He has a huge fastball, but Milwaukee's development team will be tasked with building up his nascent secondary offerings. ⚾ It's true what they say. Whether he was pitching for the Rangers or the San Antonio Missions, **Shelby Miller**'s FIP really was bigger in Texas. ⚾ The non-roster signing of **Angel Perdomo** continued the Brewers' obsession with tall pitchers—maybe they're scouting for the Bucks?—but he walked the baseline every time out and frankly didn't show much effort on the glass. ⚾ Two Tommy John surgeries later, **Drew Rasmussen** is still throwing absolute gas. The fact that he was able to complete 72 healthy innings was an accomplishment in itself, and he should reach the majors this year. ⚾ Even with just five pro starts under his belt, it's easy to see why **Ethan Small** was able to earn Pitcher of the Year honors. He finished his amateur career ranked third on the Mississippi State all-time strikeout leaderboard, and then showed his deceptive ways could miss minor-league bats just as easily. ⚾ Remember Brandon Webb? **Braden Webb** is of no relation beyond sharing a surname - a vague connection, sure, but a stronger one than the bond between his pitches and the strike zone. Webb has a mid-90s fastball and a solid curveball, yet walking seven per nine is good for nothing except getting people thinking and talking and writing about better pitchers. ⚾ **Aaron Wilkerson** went unclaimed on waivers in September, but the big guy can throw strikes and pitch long relief or spot start if needed. Now on the wrong side of 30 with a fastball too often on the wrong side of 90, it's hard to see glory in his future. ⚾ **Taylor Williams** has impressive raw stuff on paper. His fastball is a bit too straight, however, and batters hit .442 (and slugged .553) against it in 2019. ⚾ Longtime minor league ground ball savant **Eric Yardley** was finally given a chance to prove his low-velo sidearm sinker/slider routine can leave doubled-up big-leaguers slamming their helmets in frustration; it wasn't enough for him to stick with the prospect-rich Padres, but Yardley peddles a product every bullpen can use.

Brewers Prospects

The State of the System

Every year, somebody has to be the worst system in baseball. At least the big league team is good.

The Top Ten

1 Brice Turang SS   OFP: 55   ETA: 2021/22
Born: 11/21/99   Age: 20   Bats: L   Throws: R   Height: 6'0"   Weight: 173
Origin: Round 1, 2018 Draft (#21 overall)

The Report: Turang is one of a handful of Top 101 candidate shortstops this year with a good speed/glove profile, but a long horizon to an MLB role and perhaps limited offensive upside. First the good: Turang is an above-average shortstop with plus range to both sides. He's fluid with his hands and actions, and shows present good instincts on the dirt as a teenager. The arm strength is merely above-average and not a true howitzer, but he's accurate and gets it out quick.

Turang is a plus runner with strong baserunning instincts that will garner him additional value through both traditional thievery and taking the extra base. At the plate there is a potential plus hit tool. He's selective without being passive, and has a line drive swing that stays in the zone a long time. He has enough bat speed to handle better velocity and will drive balls line-to-line. Turang is wiry but not particularly projectable, so power is unlikely ever to be a major part of his game, although he will hit his fair share of doubles. If he hits .270 or .280 consistently he'll be a solid regular, but any erosion of the hit tool might make him more of a fifth infielder.

Variance: High. The lack of power might lead to him getting challenged more in the upper minors. Speed/glove combo make for a realistic bench floor, but the bat is still high variance since it's hit tool/batting average driven.

Ben Carsley's Fantasy Take: Oh god, this is where we're starting, eh? Turang's speed and positional value combine to make him a borderline top-150 dynasty prospect, but you'd be hard pressed to convince me he's more exciting than that. If it all breaks right, maybe he's pre-power Elvis Andrus, but it seems more likely he's a Jose Peraza who can actually play shortstop. Is that worth rostering? Some years. Is that worth punting a prospect roster spot for for a few seasons? It is not.

2. Tristen Lutz   OF
OFP: 55   **ETA:** 2022
Born: 08/22/98   Age: 21   Bats: R   Throws: R   Height: 6'2"   Weight: 210
Origin: Round 1, 2017 Draft (#34 overall)

The Report: Strong, athletic, and oozing *Friday Night Lights* vibes, Lutz has a lot to offer tools-wise, but you still are asking questions about how important baseball skills are developing. He's well-muscled throughout his body, and is just about completely filled out at 21. The arm is his big tool on defense, and though I think right field is his ultimate position, he covers enough ground to man center ably.

Lutz's obvious physical strength and quick bat generate at least plus raw power, but we haven't seen it in games to the extent we'd like. This is a casualty of his contact issues, currently the main weakness in his profile. The approach isn't bad, but he lacks fluidity in the box and harbors some mechanical issues that lead to swing-and-miss and suboptimal contact. Lutz sort of hunches over in the box and dips his shoulder, which results in him missing pitches up in the zone or on the outer half and popping up those that are more in his groove path. If he is going to reach this OFP, he will need to keep his K-rate from soaring against upper-level pitching and make enough good contact that his plus power plays more in games.

Variance: High. There are hit tool questions that currently hamper the efficacy of his plus power.

Ben Carsley's Fantasy Take: Lutz is the top dynasty prospect in this system for my money, but he's a scary one to invest in given the hit tool concerns. If he can make contact even slightly more frequently, he could emerge as a Hunter Renfroe-esque power-hitting OF4. If not, he profiles as more of a fourth or fifth outfielder type who'll probably commit a devastating error for the Brewers in a playoff game.

3. Aaron Ashby   LHP
OFP: 55   **ETA:** 2021
Born: 05/24/98   Age: 22   Bats: R   Throws: L   Height: 6'2"   Weight: 181
Origin: Round 4, 2018 Draft (#125 overall)

The Report: Ah, every system has to have one crafty lefty with a plus curveball, don't they? Ashby's lanky and long and excitedly brings one of the better lefty curveballs in the minors. That's something that a fairly thin pitching pipeline in Milwaukee can use. He has a clean delivery and his ability to use his limbs and tunnel his four pitches off an above-average fastball makes Ashby an exciting young prospect in a system mostly bereft of them. He needs to iron out his command issues to quiet whispers that he will be a future bullpen arm, and improving on a fringy slider and change wouldn't hurt either, but the curve is good enough that he should get every chance to start, especially in an organization that could leverage that fastball/curve combo in a more non-traditional starting pitching ways.

Variance: Medium. No real injury history and pretty filled out physically, but does need to work on command.

Ben Carsley's Fantasy Take: He's gonna get Jalen Beeks-ed, isn't he? Until Ashby is a safer bet to remain a starter, much closer to the majors or both, you needn't concern yourself with him.

4. Ethan Small   LHP

OFP: 55   ETA: 2021
Born: 02/14/97   Age: 23   Bats: L   Throws: L   Height: 6'3"   Weight: 214
Origin: Round 1, 2019 Draft (#28 overall)

The Report: It was a bit of a surprise when the Brewers popped Small at the end of the first round this past Summer. And a dry recitation of the arsenal—a fastball that sits either side of 90, a potentially average curve and solid-average change, average command of it all—well, it doesn't sound like a first round pick. The stuff is better than my rather banal description due to a very deceptive delivery and big extension from his overhead slot.

Small will vary his speed out of the windup, using big or repeated hesitations to disrupt the pitchers timing. This does limit the command projection some—although he fills up the zone—but it does put hitters off. The fastball has some riding life up and good plane down, getting far more swings and misses than a 90 mph fastball should. And he makes professional hitters look bad flailing at fringy fastball velocity. The changeup has good separation off the heater and above-average fade. The breaker is below-average at present, but will flash 50. Honestly, I don't think it's first round stuff myself, but if pitching is disrupting hitter's timing as Warren Spahn opined, Small has at least one plus-plus tool in his locker.

Variance: High. Deception isn't an out pitch. Maybe it makes the fastball one, but Small is going to have to prove it at every level.

Ben Carsley's Fantasy Take: Don't let the first-round pedigree fool you: this is a Brian Johnson-ass dynasty prospect. What's that: Johnson was a first-rounder too? As I said: you can pass.

5. Mario Feliciano   C

OFP: 55   ETA: 2021
Born: 11/20/98   Age: 21   Bats: R   Throws: R   Height: 6'1"   Weight: 195
Origin: Round 2, 2016 Draft (#75 overall)

The Report: Feliciano's potential with the bat started materializing last year, as he put up impressive numbers in High-A and showed interesting skills at the plate. He is still working on his approach, and at present has some swing/miss and strikeout issues. There's something here though, as he has a direct inside-out type swing that allows him to spray the ball to all fields and often leads to hard line drives. He will flash surprising power to all fields too, as I saw him hit several balls deep into right-center. Short and stocky-ish with plenty of strength in the lower half, Feliciano is a pretty good athlete who has the archetypical catcher's body. He is still familiarizing himself with the position, however, and how strong he ends up becoming behind the dish will have a lot to say about how his profile eventually shakes out.

Variance: High. He's begun to break out with the bat, but there are still all the risks associated with catching prospects, and he's still developing defensively.

Ben Carsley's Fantasy Take: I think the dream is that we'd value him next year the way we value Daulton Varsho now? If you think that sort of modest but meaningful ceiling is enough to consider Feliciano a top-200 dynasty prospect, I'd listen. Anything more than that and you're just encouraging me to go on another anti-catcher diatribe.

6. Carlos Rodriguez OF

OFP: 50   ETA: 2024
Born: 12/07/00   Age: 19   Bats: L   Throws: L   Height: 5'10"   Weight: 150
Origin: International Free Agent, 2017

The Report: Rodriguez has one of the more unorthodox swings you will see. He uses a hokey-pokey leg kick—you put your right foot in, you take your right foot out—that somehow doesn't lead to as many timing issues as you'd think. That said, he can get out on his front foot or out of sync, but generally the swing works well enough due to very advanced bat control and above-average, slashy bat speed. It might be the weirdest above-average hit tool I will ever project, and I'll probably never feel comfortable about it.

The 5-foot-10 listing is probably a bit generous and he's not particularly physical or projectable so any power here will be mostly of the doubles variety. Rodriguez is fast enough to stretch some of those into triples, and that speed should allow him to comfortably stick in center, although he can drift through his routes at present. It's a fairly polished up-the-middle package all in all for a teenaged outfielder, but there isn't much projection or upside, and he's a long way from the majors.

Variance: Extreme. Short-season resume only, it's kind of a wonky swing that might have issues when he sees better velocity/spin combos up the ranks.

Ben Carsley's Fantasy Take: A small teenage outfield prospect with an unorthodox yet plus hit tool and good speed? Carlos Rodriguez is Raimel Tapia, confirmed. You can add him to your watch lists, at least.

7. Corey Ray OF

OFP: 45   ETA: 2020
Born: 09/22/94   Age: 25   Bats: L   Throws: L   Height: 6'0"   Weight: 195
Origin: Round 1, 2016 Draft (#5 overall)

The Report: Third, tenth, fourth, and now back to seventh in the rankings for the former fifth overall pick in the 2016 draft. After four years, even though his ranking in the organization has ebbed and flowed, he largely remains the same player with no significant improvements. Selected as a potential five-tool player, he has failed to hit over .250 in a season with eye-popping strikeout numbers, inconsistencies playing the field and a lackluster arm. There are many who believe Ray's value might be tapped out as a fourth outfielder with pop. Coming off a successful 2018 campaign where he was the Southern League MVP and led the circuit in home runs, extra base hits, total bases, and stolen bases, 2019 got off to a rough start with a jammed finger in the first month of the season at Triple-A San Antonio. A re-aggravation of the injury shelved him for nearly six weeks and sapped the power from his swing, which relies mostly on his hips flying open to generate bat speed. The combination of holes in the swing and lack of hand strength left his offensive output close to null. Even at full health, the ceiling seems to have been lowered.

Variance: Low. He is what he mostly is. He can launch one out, swipe a bag, play left or center field, but the flaws in his game are too big to expect a consistent starting role.

Ben Carsley's Fantasy Take: It would be cruel of you to do so, but if you want to try and sell high on Ray to the guy in your fantasy league who just emerged from a three-year coma, this is probably your last chance.

8 Zack Brown   RHP   OFP: 45   ETA: 2020
Born: 12/15/94   Age: 25   Bats: R   Throws: R   Height: 6'1"   Weight: 180
Origin: Round 5, 2016 Draft (#141 overall)

The Report: After a breakout season in 2019 that saw him named Most Outstanding Pitcher in the Southern League, Brown had to take his array of mostly average stuff to the PCL. It did not go as well. Some of the wounds were self-inflicted, as Brown went through periods where he struggled to throw strikes, and Triple-A hitters could sit on and punish his low-90s fastball when it was in the zone. His curve too often was a less effective slurvy thing, and the changeup remains inconsistent, although it will flash good fade and dive even if it's firmer than you'd like. Brown's Triple-A campaign was bad enough that the Brewers left him exposed to the Rule 5 draft. But he went unselected and remains with Milwaukee. He will likely have another chance to sort himself out in the Pacific Coast League. His high effort delivery might be better suited to short bursts where the fastball can play closer to 95 and he might be able to find an above-average breaker again.

Variance: Medium. Brown's stuff isn't good enough to afford the kind of command and control wobbles he had in 2019, but he's also a good month in 2020 away from being a potential major leaguer.

Ben Carsley's Fantasy Take: A good rule of thumb is that if a dude is exposed to and unclaimed in the Rule 5 draft, you don't need to worry about his fantasy outlook.

9. Antoine Kelly   LHP   OFP: 50   ETA: 2022/23
Born: 12/05/99   Age: 20   Bats: L   Throws: L   Height: 6'6"   Weight: 205
Origin: Round 2, 2019 Draft (#65 overall)

The Report: Kelly is a big, tall lefty with a big fastball. He sits mid-90s, but has reportedly touched triple digits, and when he's going well, it looks like he's playing catch. The frame has some projection in it too, although I'd expect him to remain fairly lean. The delivery has some mechanical inconsistencies exacerbated by his tendency to throw across his body, especially out of the windup. There's a potential above-average slider here, although that takes a fair bit of squinting and projection at present. He's a cold weather JuCo arm still growing into his body, so it's going to be a bit of a project. Mid-90s velocity from a southpaw is a good place to start though.

Variance: High. There's potential power stuff from the left side, but the command and secondaries are going to need some work.

Ben Carsley's Fantasy Take: Wait, a guy with an impact fastball but poor secondaries and spotty command? Folks, it seems like maybe Antoine Kelly Has Great Stu/[is hit by a train.]

10. Devin Williams   RHP   OFP: 45   ETA: 2019
Born: 09/21/94   Age: 25   Bats: R   Throws: R   Height: 6'3"   Weight: 165
Origin: Round 2, 2013 Draft (#54 overall)

The Report: After years of injury issues including missing an entire season after Tommy John surgery, Williams finally put together a healthy season after a shift to relief and dominated the Southern League. He made a brief stop in San Antonio before spending the last two months of the year in the major league pen. Williams sits mid-90s in short bursts and can dial it up to 97-98. The pitch can pop up in the zone, but does run a bit true otherwise. His primary secondary is actually a little scroogie change that mostly works off the 10 mph velocity difference from the fastball, although Williams generally does a good job keeping it down in the zone and away from both righties and lefties. There's a slider as well. It's not true late inning or closer stuff, but Williams should have a solid career as a pen arm, perhaps as soon as this year if he can win a job in camp.

Variance: Low. It's a good fastball and he has made the majors.

Ben Carsley's Fantasy Take: Is...is Devin Williams a top-5 dynasty prospect in this system? Oh god. Make it stop.

The Next Ten

11. Drew Rasmussen   RHP
Born: 07/27/95   Age: 24   Bats: R   Throws: R   Height: 6'1"   Weight: 225
Origin: Round 6, 2018 Draft (#185 overall)

It's pretty amazing Rassmussen is back on a pro mound at all, let alone showing the stuff he did in 2019. He hadn't pitched more than 37 innings in a season since his Freshman year at Oregon State back in 2015. He's had two Tommy John surgeries in the interim, but came out in 2019 pumping mid-to-upper-90s heat past batters at three levels. Rasmussen's fastball can lack wiggle at times, but it's easy plus, bordering on plus-plus. His primary secondary is a hard, short slider he can run up to 90, and a sinking change in the upper-80s. Given his health track record, the Brewers were very cautious with his usage—while technically a starting pitcher, he never threw more than four innings or 64 pitches in an outing, and occasionally was used out of the pen to further manage his workload. The Brewers still seem interested in trying to develop him as a starter, but with this level of health risk, it almost feels like those bullets should be spent getting outs in a major league pen. Rassmussen could quickly slot into a high leverage role there too.

12 Micah Bello   OF
Born: 07/21/00   Age: 19   Bats: R   Throws: R   Height: 5'11"   Weight: 165
Origin: Round 2, 2018 Draft (#73 overall)

One of the younger prep bats available, the Brewers selected Bello in the second round of the 2018 draft. There was—and still is—plenty of baseball rawness and Milwaukee has him on a fairly conservative development track. He looks about an inch or two taller than his listed 5-foot-11 and more filled out than 165 lbs. Bello stands very upright at the plate with a medium leg kick followed by a violent uncoiling of an uppercut swing. Bello's plus bat speed makes up for some of the length, and the total package shows easy plus raw power. He's growing into a right field profile but may have the pop to match. Bello has better control of the barrel than the description of his swing implies, but the swing really only has one gear, so the hit tool may struggle against better arms. And there were already swing-and-miss and quality of contact issues against Pioneer League arms.

13 Nick Kahle   C
Born: 02/28/98   Age: 22   Bats: R   Throws: R   Height: 5'10"   Weight: 210
Origin: Round 4, 2019 Draft (#133 overall)

In a strong year for draft prospects, who finished third in the Pac-12 conference in on-base percentage behind only Adley Rutschman and Andrew Vaughn? None other than this stocky catcher from Washington selected in the fourth round. While Kahle's defensive abilities are so-so, the potential of an offensive-minded backstop with a keen eye for the zone is a welcome sight in any system. There are improvements to the swing that could be made, as he tends to get his hands locked when firing and bars out his lead arm, adding length to the bat path.

After previously struggling in wood-bat summer leagues, a strong showing in the rookie-level Pioneer League for his pro debut put to rest worries of a rough transition, before he finished his year in Hi-A.

14 — Payton Henry C
Born: 06/24/97   Age: 23   Bats: R   Throws: R   Height: 6'1"   Weight: 215
Origin: Round 6, 2016 Draft (#171 overall)

A large catcher with a strong, muscular build, Henry has long had a positive defensive reputation. 2019 looks gave us nothing that contradicts that; he moves around well behind the plate, and has enough arm to deter the running game. His standout tool at the plate is above-average power, which is a trait that will serve him well in the Fraternal Order of Backup Catchers. The problem here is with the hit tool. Henry's approach isn't great and his stiff, uphill swing results in a lot of whiffs and weak contact. There's more leeway on the offensive profile given his strong backstop defense, but he'll need to tighten things up to be a viable big league option.

15 — Joe Gray OF
Born: 03/12/00   Age: 20   Bats: R   Throws: R   Height: 6'1"   Weight: 195
Origin: Round 2, 2018 Draft (#60 overall)

Believed by many as a first-round talent entering the 2018 draft, Gray slid into the second round and hasn't had much success as a pro…yet. Despite having an idyllic baseball body with loads of projection, the rawness in his game has been exposed in the pros, especially at the plate. As a prep in Mississippi he utilized a high leg kick and decent bat-to-ball skills to feast on lesser competition. Against better velocity as a pro, the length in the swing and tardiness of his timing has left him struggling against better competition. This past season, an earnest attempt to work on his swing by switching to a stride at setup and slightly opening up did not produce better results, but with more reps using the tuned-up swing we'll see how much improvement has been made in 2020 in what will likely be his first foray into full-season ball.

16 — Cooper Hummel OF
Born: 11/28/94   Age: 25   Bats: B   Throws: R   Height: 5'10"   Weight: 198
Origin: Round 18, 2016 Draft (#531 overall)

A former catcher, the stocky 5-foot-10 outfielder possesses one of the better eyes and approaches in the Brewers system. Hummel appears very relaxed in his stance and features a leg kick that helps generate above-average power. The swing is best-suited for hunting down in the zone as he drops his hands pretty low to engage the ball. The switch-hitting Hummel doesn't really have a carrying tool—other than his eye—and his defense leaves a bit to be desired, although there is room for improvement given his lack of reps in the outfield. It's hard for ex-catchers to remain prospects after moving out from behind the dish, but if Hummel can continue to generate decent game power and work counts the way he does, he could be a platoon outfielder for the Brewers in future years.

17 Eduardo Garcia SS
Born: 07/10/02 Age: 17 Bats: R Throws: R Height: 6'2" Weight: 160
Origin: International Free Agent, 2019

Garcia was one of the big names from Milwaukee's 2018 J2 class, but went down with a fractured right ankle shortly into his Dominican Summer League debut. His carrying tool was his defense at shortstop, so how serious the ankle injury is and how his recovery goes injects even more variance into the profile of a 17-year-old who hasn't even come state side yet. We're still ranking him though, because...yeah.

18 Braden Webb RHP
Born: 04/25/95 Age: 25 Bats: R Throws: R Height: 6'3" Weight: 200
Origin: Round 3, 2016 Draft (#82 overall)

A former third-rounder out of South Carolina, the now 24-year-old Webb has struggled to gain traction in the upper levels and spent most of last year marooned at High-A. The stuff is pretty pedestrian overall, though if you squint you can see a major league arm. His fastball sits low-90s with some sink when he locates down, but his command can waver and when he leaves the fastball up it gets hit. He has three secondaries, two breakers and a sparsely-used change. His 12-6 curve is effective at generating weak contact, but it doesn't always miss bats. He'll also mix in a shorter slider in the mid-80s. The pitch mix is solid but the command still isn't there and the stuff isn't loud enough to overcome that at present.

19 Je'Von Ward OF
Born: 10/25/99 Age: 20 Bats: L Throws: R Height: 6'5" Weight: 190
Origin: Round 12, 2017 Draft (#354 overall)

If you want a, oh let's say 35th percentile outcome for Bello in 24 months, it might look a bit like Ward. Ward was also quite young for his draft class, and has a classic long and lean projectable frame even now at 20-years-old. He's taller and even toolsier than Bello but has struggled to make consistent contact do to issues with spin and a leveraged, muscley swing. His physical strength hasn't actually led to game power either, as he has hit just four home runs in 205 professional games. He's an above-average runner underway, but it can take a while for his long strides to get up to speed and he's played almost exclusively in a corner outfield spot as a pro. The chance the tools pop at some point keeps him at the back of this list, but it's one of the few he'd make.

Milwaukee Brewers 2020

20 **Lucas Erceg 3B**
Born: 05/01/95   Age: 25   Bats: L   Throws: R   Height: 6'3"   Weight: 210
Origin: Round 2, 2016 Draft (#46 overall)

This is one of those "what you see is *probably* what you get" type of guys. There's a long swing, with a sizable stride towards the mound. Unfortunately, Erceg isn't as disciplined as one would like given the below-average barrel control and length to contact. The former second-rounder's best tool is his arm, no question about it. You could tell he was a former pitcher on his throws across the diamond. And I would not be shocked to see him grade out as an average third baseman given his range and solid reads on balls to both sides. Erceg is still fairly athletic and there were some tools here in the not-so-distant past. It's a lefty bat with potential 20+ homers. You can find a place for that, but there is a lot of work still to do to get there for a guy in Triple-A.

Personal Cheeseball

PC **Max Lazar RHP**
Born: 06/03/99   Age: 21   Bats: R   Throws: R   Height: 6'3"   Weight: 185
Origin: Round 11, 2017 Draft (#324 overall)

Back during one of Carlos Tocci's three seasons in Lakewood, Jarrett Seidler coined the term "jeans buddy" to describe his physique. This is a prospect that could wear the same jeans size as me, and as I'm presently around a 30/32, this isn't generally the frame or physicality you find in future major leaguers. There have been several since, usually undersized, lean, sometimes projectable position players. Nick Gordon is the best present example. They aren't usually pitchers, but Max Lazar might fit. I'd have to roll the cuffs since he is listed at 6-foot-3, but the uniform literally hangs off the 20-year-old. Nevertheless, he can dial it up into the low-90s, but sits more upper-80s. There's low spin, creating some sink. He has a potentially average change and a fringy, mid-70s breaker. He throws strikes with everything and it was more than enough to overwhelm A-ball at first time of asking, which I guess is more than Carlos Tocci could say. Lazar has some projection left and will have to add more strength and velocity though, as the overall stuff profile is a bit underwhelming at present.

Low Minors Sleeper

LMS **Nick Bennett LHP**
Born: 09/01/97   Age: 22   Bats: L   Throws: L   Height: 6'4"   Weight: 210
Origin: Round 6, 2019 Draft (#193 overall)

The sixth round of the draft is a bit deeper than we'd normally go for a low minors sleeper, but you have probably figured out by now that this Brewers system is pretty thin. Bennett's a sturdy college southpaw with a high-spin fastball around 90. There's some lefty funk and deception that helps the pitch play up without significantly impacting his ability to throw strikes. His mid-70s 1-7 curve has average projection and comes in at a tough angle for lefties to deal with. There's some risk he's just a LOOGY in an era of baseball where that role has been functionally eliminated, but the curve may be good enough to cross over.

Top Talents 25 and Under (as of 4/1/2020)

1. Keston Hiura
2. Josh Hader
3. Luis Urias
4. Corbin Burnes
5. Brice Turang
6. Eric Lauer
7. Tristen Lutz
8. Aaron Ashby
9. Ethan Small
10. Freddy Peralta

The Brewers organization got sneaky old rather quickly, and they're now trying to fill multiple big-league holes with major-league veterans on short contracts because the farm system has dried up after some trades and promotions. Hader has proven himself to be one of the most dominant relievers in baseball, striking out almost 50 percent of opposing batters and posting 2.6- and 2.7-win seasons in 2018 and 2019, respectively. Still, Hiura hit .303/.368/.570 in his big-league debut. Even with questionable defense, he would've matched Hader's WARP over the course of an entire season. Hiura is more valuable to the Brewers than Hader due to the fact that Hiura is younger, has more years of control, and has less risk (before you argue, consider Edwin Díaz in 2019). Regardless, it's a nice one-two punch to have atop a 25U list, especially given modern bullpen usage.

Things then crater in a hurry. Luis Urias has the prospect pedigree and the bat-to-ball skills to be a significant big-league contributor at shortstop, but he simply hasn't hit the ball very hard in the majors. Perhaps he develops a bit more strength—as Urias is only 22 years old—but guys who rely on a premium hit tool and show up with below-average exit velocities aren't safe prospects. Luckily, he's there to replace Orlando Arcia, who was the second-worst hitter among qualified hitters in 2019 and was second-worst among hitters with at least 300 PA in 2018. Urias will get his chances.

After Urias, the Brewers have a mix of guys who either are safe but unexciting, or are exciting but have gone through bouts of being absolutely terrible. Burnes represents the latter. He cruised through the Brewers' minor-league system and performed well in his big-league debut out of the bullpen in 2018, posting a 2.61

ERA with a 3.39 DRA. The right-hander followed that up with a dumpster fire of a season, in which he served up 17 homers in just 49 innings and had an 8.82 ERA. His performance raised questions about his repertoire, particularly his fastball and its spin, to the point that the Brewers sent him to their "pitching lab" in Maryvale during the summer to work things out. He's a massive question mark heading into 2020 and beyond.

Brice Turang and Eric Lauer are your safe-but-unexciting guys. They have useful, high floors, but come with physical limitations that will be difficult to overcome. Turang hasn't posted an ISO above .090—ya know, in case you thought the questions about his power are overstated—while Lauer is your quintessential back-end lefty who doesn't throw hard and doesn't miss many bats. He's the left-handed version of Zach Davies, for those who regret Davies' move to San Diego. Safe but unexciting.

Lutz perhaps offers the best impact potential amongst the Brewers' bats in the upper reaches of the organization's minor-league system, but he's a 21-year-old power-hitting corner outfielder who has never hit more than 13 homers in a season. He also has holes in his swing. Ashby is a left-handed curveball specialist who saw his strikeout rate nosedive upon reaching High-A, which makes one wonder if his dynamic deuce is good enough on its own to overcome control issues. Hitters at the upper levels might just force him to throw strikes with his fastball. As for Small, he's a Trackman Superstar who seemingly finds way more success than his raw stuff would otherwise indicate. If you're looking for a potential breakout, Small is your guy. The lefty just has no professional track record to quiet those who raised an eyebrow when the Brewers popped him in the first round.

Peralta has been a volatile pitcher for the Brew Crew. He tossed eight shutout innings and struck out 11 against the Pirates on April 3 and subsequently coughed up seven earned runs in 3 1/3 innings his next time out against the Angels. After moving to the bullpen late in 2019, though, Peralta may have found his role. His fastball velocity jumped to 96.22 mph, and he struck out 52.6 percent of the batters he faced in September. The righty followed up that performance by striking out 23 batters in 6 2/3 innings down in the Dominican Winter League, reportedly hitting 98 mph on the gun. If the Brewers commit to him as a reliever, he could be a multi-inning weapon to pair with Hader as early as 2020. The small sample and aforementioned volatility, though, keep him low on the list. After all, we've done this song and dance with Peralta before many times.

Part 3: Featured Articles

The Baseball Is Juiced (Again)

Robert Arthur

This article originally appeared at Baseball Prospectus on April 5, 2019.

It started when the normally reliable Chris Sale got lit up for three homers by the Mariners in the Red Sox's season opener. It was part of a record number of taters that flew on Opening Day, as starters from Sale to Zack Greinke were taken deep by the handful. Then Christian Yelich hit a home run in each of his first four games, tying yet another MLB record, this one for consecutive games with a dinger to start a season.

It didn't take long for fans and players to begin whispering and tweeting about the baseballs being juiced again. It's early yet for us to come to any definitive conclusion about the 2019 season, but preliminary data shows that the baseball has returned to its aerodynamic peak. Whether that means this season will smash home run records like 2017 did remains to be seen.

Before home run explosion over the last few years, no one worried too much about the baseball's air resistance. While MLB and Rawlings (the company that manufactures the official baseballs) kept track of dozens of metrics to make sure that the ball was consistent from month to month, they didn't measure drag.

But drag is incredibly important in determining how likely a hitter is to knock one out of the park. As baseballs become more aerodynamic, they travel further given a certain initial velocity. A deep fly ball that might have been caught at the warning track can instead go into the first row of the stands. A three percent change in drag coefficient can work to add about five feet to a well-hit fly ball, which can in turn increase home runs league wide by an astounding 10-15 percent.

It's possible to measure the aerodynamics of the baseball using the pitch-tracking radars currently in place in each MLB ballpark. By calculating the loss of speed from when the pitch is released to when it crosses the plate, you can directly measure the drag coefficient on the baseball. I first wrote about the role of decreasing drag in boosting home runs in 2017, and MLB's commission of scientists and statisticians later confirmed that the more aerodynamic baseballs

Milwaukee Brewers 2020

in use that year were largely to blame for the spike in home runs. The same commission rejected some alternate hypotheses, like rising temperatures and a league-wide boost in launch angle pushing more balls over the fence.

The current era has featured some large fluctuations in drag coefficient, leading to first an explosion in 2016 and 2017, and then a dialing back of homers last year. Curious about the record-breaking home run tallies in the last few days, I used the same methodology to measure the aerodynamics of the baseballs so far in 2019.

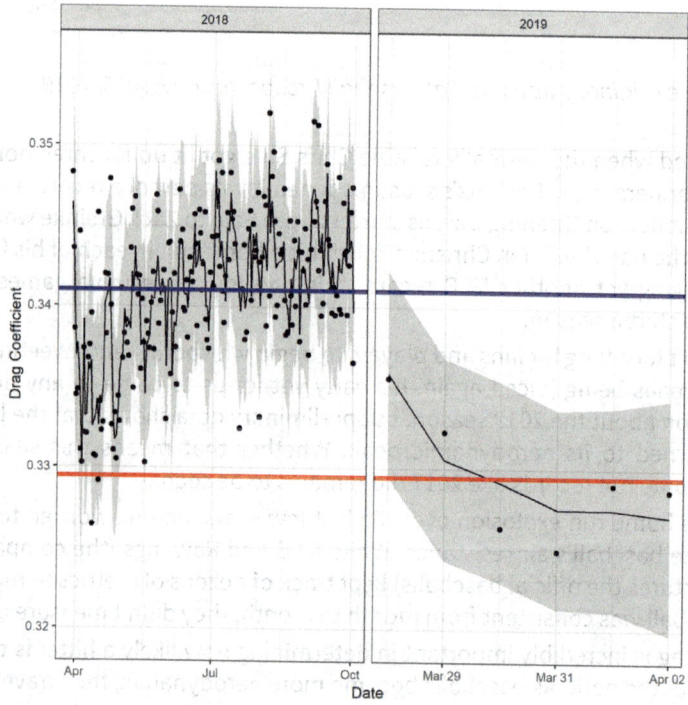

We're only a week into the 2019 season, but the drag numbers so far are among the lowest recorded in the last calendar year. With apologies for gory math, the current 2019 season average drag coefficient (the red line) would be below the 95 percent credible interval (the shaded area) for about nine-tenths of the 2018 season. (I used a Bayesian Random Walk model implemented in INLA to calculate these credible intervals, averaging the drag numbers in each game and adjusting for park.)

There were only a handful of six-day stretches in 2018 that had drag numbers below what we're seeing now, and most were in late June and early July. All of this means that 2019's data so far is quite a bit different than what we saw through most of last year.

These drag coefficients factor out the effects of temperature and air density, so they aren't a product of April cold. However, the numbers could be deceptive if the radars used to track pitches have changed from year to year. I consulted with some experts within baseball who were not aware of any specific modifications to the radar this year that could produce this pattern, but it's an important caveat of which to be aware.

On the one hand, it's only been six days, and we don't quite have the statistical basis to say that these drag coefficients are unprecedented compared to 2018. On the other hand, we've witnessed about 5,000 fastballs so far this season, so it's not as if our sample size is small. At least so far, the baseball has played like it's much more aerodynamic than it was last year. In fact, the current drag coefficient is really only comparable to 2017, when the baseballs were more aerodynamic than they had been in at least a decade.

It's not just fancy radar tracking indicating that the baseball is flying through the air more easily. The current number of home runs per game (as of this writing) is the highest it's been since the heady days of 2017, the year that teams and players broke dinger-related records everywhere you looked. That's especially remarkable considering that we're in what is typically the coldest part of the regular season, when lower temperatures and higher winds tend to suppress offense and keep balls in the air within the park. Comparing only from April to April, this year's rate of home runs per fly ball is even a little bit higher than it was in 2017.

With that said, the current measurements are no guarantee that 2019 will be another year of record-shattering homer hitting. The trouble with the drag measurements is that they are not consistent from June to August, from week to week, or even sometimes from day to day. Whether because of natural manufacturing variation or differences in the underlying supplies of cowhide and thread that go into the baseballs, drag has a tendency to fluctuate up and down over the course of a year. So the homers that fly in the first week of April wouldn't necessarily clear the fence a week later.

It's possible that this one-week drop in drag coefficient subsides and the baseball returns to its 2018 levels. On the other hand, it's almost equally probable that the ball becomes even more slippery and flies ever farther. Either way, it's clear that the baseball's air resistance is something to keep an eye on for the remainder of the 2019 season.

—*Robert Arthur is an author of Baseball Prospectus.*

The Moral Hazard of Playing It Safe

Craig Goldstein

This article originally appeared at Baseball Prospectus on August 6, 2019.

A couple days prior to the trade deadline, amidst a sea of tranquility posing as the lead up to the trade deadline, Bob Nightengale took to Twitter. Nightengale, who was probably wearing his pants backwards at the time, tweeted that MLB GMs were coming around on the idea that the unified trade deadline should be moved back from July 31 to August 15, so they could better assess their positions in the standings and whether they should buy or sell. To which I said:

This might strike some as reductive and churlish. And it might be that, but it isn't really wrong, either. Jeff Quinton wrote a great piece discussing the environmental factors that enable front offices to avoid risk without upsetting the apple cart within their own fanbases. I don't believe that it goes far enough, however. His article gives us the proper framework through which to understand why these behaviors have been allowed to seep into front offices throughout the league. Understanding the reasons behind these actions are different from excusing them, though, and GMs should not be let off the hook for their non-competitive approach to the trade deadline (much less the offseason).

⚾ ⚾ ⚾

It's fair to say that fans as a group have rarely, if ever, been pro-player. It is also fair to say that in the time during and following the Moneyball revolution, the pendulum swung from fans who cared intensely about winning in the moment (and thus might be intolerant of a rebuilding approach) to fans who supported building a team that could compete throughout multiple seasons, viewing the playoffs as a crapshoot, with the thought that getting multiple bites at the apple was a better approach than taking a bigger bite in any one season.

There's nothing wrong with that approach, and I still find merit in that argument. However, it seems that the pendulum has swung too far in that direction. Teams are overvaluing some of the individual factors that make themselves long-term contenders rather than attempting to seize a championship when given the opportunity. It's a difficult needle to thread.

And surely, they (and those in similar positions) would have liked another two weeks to clarify where they stand so as to better marshal their resources. We've all asked for a few more minutes when staring at a menu. But all of these GMs and front office personnel are where they are to make difficult decisions. They have proprietary data and internal analysts dedicated to understanding their position relative to the rest of the league, and how any move in the here and now impacts their long-term vision. To complain (if that report is accurate) that over half the season is not enough to properly assess their season is bullshit of the highest order. Move the deadline, and you'd simply have increasingly discounted trade offers because teams would be acquiring even less control of anyone they're acquiring, rental or not.

Major league front offices are behaving like the managers they lampooned two decades ago. They're effectively sacrificing a runner to second in the ninth inning—not because it's the correct move, but rather because it is safe. It used to be that the phrase "moral hazard" was used to describe general managers who made ill-fated, short-sighted decisions aimed at locking in wins and securing their jobs at the expense of their team's future. Now, general managers are guilty of committing moral hazards in the opposite direction, playing it utterly safe and terrified of becoming scapegoats.

In lieu of bold action, they opt to pussyfoot around a current window of contention, choosing instead to play the long game and stack up years of control like they're blocks in a game of Jenga. GMs pass on signing quality players in free agency because the back-end of the deal might look bad, and because they might be able to squeeze out 70 percent of the production from a player who costs a tenth as much. That's a safer investment, too, because it's also hard to prove a negative—it's impossible to prove that Manny Machado would make the Mets a playoff team in 2019-2020, but it's easy to say that the back half of Robinson Cano's contract sucks. Owners, who rule over GM's jobs, are also humans with human brain processes that will always make the so-called albatross contract uglier than the road not taken.

These days, GMs are remembered for the bad deals they make and the surplus value they generate, not the acquisition of expensive, necessary talents that meet their market worth (or fall slightly short while still providing significant on-field value). And front offices know that one or two expensive misfires can cost them their jobs, no matter how many good deals they make.

No front office exemplifies this ethos more than the Toronto Blue Jays. General Manager Ross Atkins had this to say following the Blue Jays underwhelming trade deadline:

This is by no means the first time that an executive will cite years of control to justify their actions, which is often just another way of saying "don't look at what we got, look at how much we got of it." Atkins touts quantity to elide the discussion of quality—either, that of the players acquired, or those given up. Remember: the other teams presumably value years of control, too.

Atkins also had some thoughts to offer regarding free agents back in early 2018:

This ignores, of course, whether the player can create enough value in the front end of a contract to justify the longer term of a deal, and the decline that often occurs in the back end. It also ignores whether the player can fill a need the team requires and put them in a position to compete for and win a championship. But as teams seemingly avoid contention at all, where they might end up having to consider and later justify some of these tough decisions, we still see risk-averse approaches.

Anthony Fenech's article on two trades that recently extended GM Al Avila didn't make got at this issue rather well:

> Passing on those deals was defensible: Both players had yet to break out and trading [Michael] Fulmer—a pitcher who appeared to be a future ace, no matter his injury concerns—would have taken serious gumption, opening Avila up to strong criticism.

Avoiding strong criticism is something each of us can understand as a motivation, but the avoidance of criticism only matters if that criticism is valid. In Fulmer's case, shoving his injury concerns aside affects not only the years that the team controls him (he is currently missing a full season due to Tommy John surgery) but also the quality of those seasons, as his knee and elbow injuries combined to dampen his effectiveness even when healthy enough to pitch. But it was easy to present the then-current image of Fulmer as a top of the rotation pitcher who the team had under its domain for the next five seasons as something to build around. The status quo isn't nearly as often second-guessed as a decision that disrupts it.

⚾ ⚾ ⚾

MLB GMs are risk-averse to a fault. They are ivy-educated and consulting firm-approved, and yet they can't seem to avoid leaving wins on the table in their all-consuming lust for a non-existent $/WAR championship. They are supposed to zig when everyone else zags, and not merely pay lip service to the idea of zigging through a calculated PR plan built on convincing the fan base their approach is novel when it actually apes most of their competitors. Instead they've become far more concerned with making safe, accepted-by-the-new-common-wisdom decisions, such that our prior understanding of what a moral hazard is has become inverted.

I can't blame them entirely, and not only because of the reasons that Quinton illuminated in his article, but also because of the damage wrought by the introduction of the second wild card (WC2) spot. MLB's desire to have more teams in playoff contention has sparked anti-competitive behavior. Teams know now that they do not need to swing big as they assemble their roster because there is a good chance that a mediocre team can either catch fire and capture a division, or muddle along until they back into the WC2.

Simultaneously, the one-game playoff has neutered the WC1, putting an entire season on the flip of a coin like some sort of baseball-obsessed Anton Chigurh. While the one-game playoff makes sense as a way to increase the value of winning a division, it also means that if a front office doesn't like its chances of overcoming a behemoth like the Dodgers or Astros in the offseason, they have few incentives to chase glory. Similarly, the relative inaction in the NL Central at the trade deadline—despite a wide open division—can be explained by the idea that any high-variance investment could still result in only a wild card (or worse) result, given the mere two months left in the season to make an impact.

⚾ ⚾ ⚾

As stated at the top, we should not confuse reasons for excuses. The implementation of the second wild card is just one of many environmental factors that influence how each front office operates. I am convinced that it is one of the larger factors, but I am also convinced that organizations need to shed the yoke of "efficiency at all costs" so that they can instead pursue competition, as the spirit of the game intends. Until they do, we're all deadline losers.

—*Craig Goldstein is an author of Baseball Prospectus.*

Index of Names

Abreu, Pablo 91
Albers, Matt 52
Anderson, Brett 54
Arcia, Orlando 20
Ashby, Aaron 86, 96
Bello, Micah 91, 101
Bennett, Nick 104
Black, Ray 56
Braun, Ryan 22
Brown, Zack 93, 99
Broxton, Keon 24
Burnes, Corbin 58
Cain, Lorenzo 26
Claudio, Alex 60
Dillard, Thomas 91
Erceg, Lucas 80, 104
Ernesto, Larry 91
Faria, Jacob 93
Feliciano, Mario 81, 97
Feyereisen, J.P. 93
Freitas, David 91
Gamel, Ben 28
García, Avisaíl 30
Garcia, Eduardo 103
Gray, Joe 102
Guerra, Deolis 93
Hader, Josh 62
Healy, Ryon 91
Henry, Payton 91, 102
Hiura, Keston 32
Houser, Adrian 64
Hummel, Cooper 102
Jackson, Jay 93
Jeffress, Jeremy 93
Kahle, Nick 91, 101
Kelly, Antoine 93, 100
Knebel, Corey 87
Lauer, Eric 66
Lazar, Max 104
Lindblom, Josh 88
Lutz, Tristen 91, 96
Mathias, Mark 91
Miller, Shelby 93
Morin, Mike 68
Narváez, Omar 34
Nottingham, Jacob 82
Peralta, Freddy 70
Perdomo, Angel 93
Peterson, Jace 91
Phelps, David 72
Piña, Manny 36
Rasmussen, Drew 93, 100
Ray, Corey 83, 98
Rodriguez, Carlos 91, 98
Rodríguez, Ronny 38
Saladino, Tyler 40
Small, Ethan 93, 97
Smoak, Justin 42
Sogard, Eric 44
Spangenberg, Cory 46
Supak, Trey 89
Suter, Brent 74

Milwaukee Brewers 2020

Taylor, Tyrone 84
Turang, Brice 85, 95
Urías, Luis 48
Wahl, Bobby 90
Ward, Je'Von 103
Webb, Braden 93, 103
Wilkerson, Aaron 93
Williams, Devin 76, 100
Williams, Taylor 93
Woodruff, Brandon 78
Yardley, Eric 93
Yelich, Christian 50